Cambridge
Newspapers
and
Opinion
1780-1850

Cambridge Newspapers and Opinion 1780-1850

Michael J. Murphy

THE OLEANDER PRESS OF CAMBRIDGE

The Oleander Press
17 Stansgate Avenue
Cambridge CB2 2QZ

The Oleander Press
210 Fifth Avenue
New York, N.Y. 10010

ISBN 0 900891 15 7

British Library Cataloguing in Publication Data

Murphy, Michael Joseph
    Cambridge newspapers and opinion, 1780-1850.
    – (Cambridge town, gown and county; vol. 12).
    1. English newspapers – England – Cambridge –
    History
    I. Title II. Series
    072'.6'59   PN5129.C/

Designed by Ron Jones

Printed and bound by The Burlington Press, Foxton

Contents

Illustrations

Acknowledgements

I wish to thank Donald Read who has been a stimulating mentor in the field of newspaper history; E.P. Thompson and E.A. Smith for useful suggestions which I have incorporated in the section on Benjamin Flower; my colleagues Piers Brendon and Anthony Kirby; Michael J. Petty and the staff of the Cambridgeshire Collection; the staff of the Cambridge University Library and the British Museum Newspaper Library, Colindale; and finally my wife Valerie for her general help and unfailing encouragement.

Permission to reproduce illustrations was given by Miss H.E. Peek, Keeper of the Archives, Cambridge University Library; M.J. Petty, A.L.A. Local Studies Librarian, Cambridgeshire Collection; and V. Lennox-Key of the Lindsey Press. The author and publishers express their thanks for the granting of such permission.

Foreword

'Few things are sought with more eagerness, few things are sooner cast aside as worthless than a newspaper.' These remarks about the ephemeral nature of newspapers, made in the 1850s still, of course, apply as far as ordinary readers are concerned. Until recently even historians were slow to treat newspapers seriously as significant influences upon, and expressions of, public opinion. Newspapers were used as quarries of factual evidence, either for national or local history, but only *The Times* was regarded as important in its own right. Its official history appeared in five volumes between 1935 and 1952. During the last twenty-five years, however, the study of English newspaper opinion has taken on a new breadth and sophistication. It is still too soon to write a serious general history of the national or provincial press; but A.J. Lee has offered a valuable interim analysis of *The Origins of the Popular Press, 1855-1914* (1976). The *Manchester Guardian* long played a unique part as both a local and a national newspaper, and it was especially valuable to have its career perceptively charted and analysed in David Ayerst's *Guardian: biography of a newspaper* (1971). But studies are still needed of such influential national papers as the *Daily Telegraph* — the big success story among mid-Victorian papers; or the *Daily Mail* — the exemplar of Harmsworth's 'new journalism'. Nevertheless, about twenty theses on nineteenth-century English newspaper history have now been completed — listed in S.P. Bell's *Dissertations on British History, 1815-1914* (1974) — several of which I have myself enjoyed the privilege either of supervising or of examining. A number have been published as books, including one valuable regional study, Maurice Milne's *Newspapers of Northumberland and Durham* (1971).

My own *Press and People 1790-1850: opinion in three English cities* (1961), showed what might be attempted by way of comparison between the newspapers of three cities (Manchester, Leeds, and Sheffield). Michael Murphy's present volume has applied and adapted some of the techniques of enquiry used in that book to the newspaper history of a very different type of place in the same period. The text has been substantially revised from his University of Kent M.A. thesis (1971); and he now offers a very readable account, of interest not only to scholars but to anyone with a care for history in the making at the grass roots.

The years from the end of the eighteenth century to the middle of the nineteenth witnessed the first impact of the Industrial Revolution upon English society and politics, an impact which could not be ignored in the agricultural

7

districts. Could the social and political balance be adjusted gradually and peacefully? Or would the new industrial middle and working classes break out in violent revolution, either because of their own impetuosity or because of inadequate response to their problems and aspirations from the landed interest, which had traditionally dominated both the social and political systems? These were the big national questions from the days of the younger Pitt to the days of the younger Peel. At the local level the Industrial Revolution brought the opportunity for 'improvements' (to use the contemporary word), especially in communication of goods and people – better roads, new canals, and eventually railways. Promotion of, and opposition to, such innovations became an important part of local politics even in places far distant from the mills and furnaces of the industrial districts.

The part played by the Cambridge press in rallying and reflecting local public opinion on such local and national issues is discussed by Michael Murphy clearly and judiciously, and at the right level of selected detail. Cambridge was not only an important country town but also one of the two university centres, and its reactions therefore possess an especial significance in terms of national opinion. Moreover, the career of Benjamin Flower, editor of the *Cambridge Intelligencer,* was of national importance. Flower, who has been half-forgotten since his own day, now emerges as an important early Radical and as one of the great pioneers of English journalism, who spoke to a national readership from a local base. In Michael Murphy's words, at the height of the French Revolution in 1793 Flower 'set out to instruct public opinion by reporting parliamentary proceedings and political meetings, and, much more important, by criticising party and authority through powerfully-worded editorial articles. The *Intelligencer* was the first provincial newspaper in England to develop these new techniques and continue them for an appreciable length of time.'

How much influence Flower and other newspaper editors, national and local, were able to exert will always remain uncertain. It was often remarked that they could reinforce a tendency of opinion but could not create or prevent one. In 1870 Leslie Stephen compared press influence with the process of natural selection. 'It is constantly raising all manner of discordant and disconnected war-cries. If they happen to fall in with the humour of the time, a general rush is made with immense vigour in the direction indicated. If they do not meet with sympathy they drop out of notice.' In 1892 Gladstone looked back over the nineteenth century, and concluded that 'three P's have denoted the instruments by which British Freedom has been principally developed and confirmed. These three P's are PETITION, PRESS, and PLATFORM.' The history of petitioning and of public meetings has already begun to be written; but it will need to be set alongside that of the press before the origins and effects of 'public opinion' can be seen in the round. We may then be much closer to knowing not only what men of the nineteenth century did but what they thought. The two can then be related to tell us why men acted as they did, and what men thought they were doing by their actions.

DONALD READ

1
Town, County and University in the Eighteenth Century

I

By the end of the eighteenth century almost every part of Georgian England from the smallest country parish to the largest factory town, bore witness to the changing nature of English urban and rural life. England was being transformed from an agricultural society based on the plough and the loom to an industrial democracy standing proudly, if a little uncertainly, on her new industries and new resources. The impact of this industrial and social revolution varied. Many of the older towns such as Oxford and Cambridge slumbered on, devoid of industrial resources and cushioned by the privileges, and incomes, of members of the aristocracy and the Church. A traveller approaching Cambridge in 1790 would have been impressed by the essentially rural nature of the setting: 'Modern Cambridge is situate in a fine fruitful Plain, on the river Grant. Extensive Cornfields on the South . . . and on the North-east, are fruitful Meadows, extending as far as the Eye can reach . . . from the West . . . beautiful Colleges, Groves, Gardens and green Fields lying on the Banks of the River . . .'[1] Wordsworth as a young undergraduate was more excited by the stimulating atmosphere of the town itself:

I was the Dreamer, they the Dream; I roam'd
Delighted, through the motley spectacle;
Gowns grave or gaudy, Doctors, Students, Streets,
Lamps, Gateways, Flocks of Churches, Courts and Towers . . .[2]

This is not surprising. Cambridge was after all a historic university town which still retained much of its mediaeval character. It had less than 10,000 inhabitants and had hardly grown beyond its ancient limits. Yet, in spite of the cloistered architectural beauty of its colleges, the general appearance of the town was certainly less pleasing than one might have anticipated. The streets were narrow and winding and the houses were in many instances old, badly built, and crowded closely together. They stretched along a line from Castle Hill in the north, over Magdalene Bridge, past the Round Church, around the old Market Place and southwards along Trumpington Street. Though the highways leading to the town were in a tolerable condition, the streets in the town were dirty, unlighted and unpaved. Gutters were often in the middle of the road; spouts discharged from roofs on to the heads of pedestrians and shop fronts had been extended so far, by projecting windows, that in many of the streets two carriages could not pass each other.[3] In the universal darkness of the winter evenings, bands of under-graduates carrying lighted torches often roamed the town. They intimidated passers-by, insulting them and taking their lanterns from them 'and occasioned great terror and apprehensions that some parts of the colleges or town may be fired thereby.'[4] However, very little desire was evinced by the Corporation or the inhabitants for improving the town by cleansing, paving and lighting. Many considered the advantages of such improvements doubtful and a heavy expenditure certain. Others felt that if town lighting was introduced fights between undergraduates and townspeople would recur on a larger scale 'As now persons, not being able to recognise each other in the dark, more frequently passed without quarrelling.'[5]

Like Oxford, Cambridge was founded because it was well situated. A place where road and river traffic can readily meet is an obvious stopping-point for loading and unloading, doing business, building warehouses, shops and inns. It was the gateway to the eastern counties and easily accessible from London, the North-East and the East Midlands. During the eighteenth century therefore, county notables and speculators displayed a certain interest in forming Turnpike Trusts to deal in particular with the section of the Great North Road that ran through the county, and also to improve other major roads, many of which were often impassable in winter. Details of these Trusts are given by Cooper in his *Annals of Cambridge* and many advertisements concerning them appeared regularly in the local press.[6] By the 1790s, coaches bearing such names as 'The Telegraph', 'The Union' and the well-known 'Fly', were taking people to London in eight hours, at a cost of ten to twelve shillings, leaving from such popular inns as The Red Lion in Petty Cury, The Rose in the Market Place, The Hoop in Bridge Street, and The Bell on Peas Hill.[7] In 1837 ten different coaches left Cambridge for London every day of the week and others ran to Oxford and Birmingham, as well as the more important towns of East Anglia. The last stage coach set out from Cambridge to London in 1849.[8]

Proposals were also put forward to link the Cam with the Thames, by way of Bishop's Stortford, but due to opposition from the Corporation and the conservators of the Cam, these came to nothing.[9] Suggested railway projects were also resisted from 1835 to 1842, and the town had to wait until 1845 for its first railway link (with Norwich), which was opened by the Great Eastern Railway Company.[10] This lack of sympathy for progressive improvements was typical of the town in the late eighteenth century. There are many reasons for the comparative stagnation of Cambridge at this time. Dominated by the University and dependent on its immediate countryside it remained very local in its outlook.[11] It had no native industries, the wool trade had long declined and deserted the area and even Stourbridge Fair was falling into decay. The result was that Cambridge's trade and its tradesmen suffered. However the French Wars of the 1790s proved to be a turning point and for a short time the consequent stimulus to agriculture had a beneficial effect on the town and district.

Cambridge experienced a substantial increase in population in the first forty years of the nineteenth century. During this period town population grew from about 10,000 to 24,500, the centre of the town rapidly becoming over-crowded.[12] This aggravated existing problems of health, housing and sanitation. Enclosure acts in 1801, 1807 and 1811 relieved some of the resultant congestion and a rapid expansion of building followed in the old area of open fields, especially towards Newmarket. The University also increased considerably in size after 1800, and the subsequent increase in the number of undergraduates (its resident population during term time now numbering about two thousand) helped expand trade and employment.[13] Evidence of town improvement is confirmed by an act in 1788 which set up a body of Paving Commissioners empowered to cleanse, pave and light the town. A few minor improvements followed; Petty Cury, the first street to be paved with rounded cobbles, was completed in 1793 at a cost of £23,814; oil lamps were fixed to the walls of colleges and houses and two roadside runnels were constructed in Trumpington Street to replace the dangerous stream in the middle of the road.[14]

The town also acquired a hospital in the eighteenth century from the legacy of John Addenbrooke, a fellow of St. Catharine's Hall, and after its foundation gentlemen of the University and the county subscribed the necessary funds to enable it to continue.[15] The town had its share of the major social problems of the day, the most pressing being vagrancy. Numerous open villages and wide stretches of fen invited all kinds of itinerants and the two Cambridge fairs also brought in their train an idle and disease-ridden rabble. In addition the town was on the northern route from London via Royston, through which town passed a host of wanderers and vagrants making their way to and from the metropolis. In 1820 some seven thousand vagrants entered or left Cambridge by this route alone, and the numbers continued to swell during the next decade.[16] In Cambridge only a fifth of town paupers were in the parish workhouses in 1804. The overwhelming majority continued to receive outdoor relief. By the early thirties their numbers had trebled and the resultant complaints about costs and rates encouraged the rethinking that produced the Poor Law Amendment Act of 1834.[17]

The economic importance of Cambridge at this time, as has been suggested, turned on its position as a centre of communications. It was the chief marketing area for the county, and served as a clearing house for the agricultural produce of the surrounding countryside, whilst its accessibility from so many directions still made it an ideal venue for Stourbridge and Midsummer Fairs. The continuing importance of these fairs as a source of tolls and rents is indicated by the fact that Stourbridge Fair was opened in state by the Mayor and Corporation until 1790, and both fairs continued to be well-attended by members of the town, county and University.[18] For a description of Stourbridge Fair, one cannot do better than turn to Defoe, who visited the fair when it was at its height in the early eighteenth century.[19] Wool, iron ware, coal, wines, fish, brass, glass and hops were sold there in enormous quantities. All sorts of traders, dealers and retailers visited the fair, so that not only Cambridge but all the towns around were full of merchants and travellers. Barns and stables were turned into inns to accommodate them, and an enormous demand for provisions arose.

However, first in importance came the river-borne trade. From mediaeval times until 1845, when the opening of the railway to London dealt the river trade a heavy blow, the waterway from Cambridge to the Wash was one of the main thoroughfares of trade in the Eastern Midlands. King's Lynn was in fact 'the port' of Cambridge until the mid-nineteenth century: 'The Cam happily secures an extensive trade in coals and corn, particularly oats and barley. Great quantities of oil, pressed by the numerous mills in the Isle of Ely, from flax, hemp and coleseed are brought up the Cam. A great quantity of butter is likewise conveyed every week from Norfolk and the Isle of Ely and sent by Cambridge wagons to London where it obtains the name of Cambridge butter.'[20] In 1749, over two thousand firkins of this butter, principally from Norfolk, was being loaded every Monday morning at Great Bridge Quay and sent thence to London by wagon. Most of the corn which went to King's Lynn was then sent by sea to London for the victualling of that city.[21] Cambridge in return received mostly coal, iron, stone timber and fish from the port. The town therefore continued to be an important market centre. In the market, which stands on one of the oldest sites in the borough, fish, poultry, butter, fruit and vegetables were sold, and livestock also on the outskirts of the town. The old street names are evidence of the trades plied in the town – Butchery Row, Hog Hill, Tanner's Hall, Potter's Row, Butter Row, and many others. 'Underneath the Shire Hall the butchers have their stalls on Saturdays, which is the grand market day', but there was a market every day in the town for poultry and butter.[22] Although few manufactured goods were produced in the area, the town, because of the University, gave rise to a particular number of specialised industries. Printers could find a ready market and source of employment in Cambridge. One such famous printer in the late eighteenth century was John Bowtell. He had a flourishing business as a printer and bookbinder, was a retail seller of books and prints, and was also employed as binder to the Cambridge University Library. He is particularly famed for the discovery of what was apparently the first effective substitute for leather in bookbinding.[23] University printing was carried on exclusively at the University Press buildings in Silver Street in the eighteenth century and transferred to the new Pitt Press buildings in 1833.

In the county industry was, of course, completely subordinate to agriculture; there were few towns of note in the area besides Cambridge. Saffron was grown abundantly throughout the county in the eighteenth century; timber at Wisbech continued to be an important industry in the nineteenth century, also sugar from the beet root, brewing from barley and malt and the manufacture of agricultural implements.[24] Quarrying, brickmaking, and pottery were fostered after the linking of Cambridge to London by railway in 1845. In general however agriculture predominated, yet even here the picture was not very encouraging at the close of the eighteenth century. Poverty and unemployment existed in the exaggerated form assumed in predominantly agricultural regions under the old Poor Law and poor rates were alarmingly high.[25] The total area of the county was estimated by Charles Vancouver in 1794 at about 443,000 acres.[26] Of this about 150,000 acres were waste and unimproved fen, and almost the same amount was open field arable. So almost two-thirds of the county was either unproductive or it produced little. There were two major problems reflected in these figures — the first was the need for improved drainage and the second the need for increased enclosure of open fields and better utilisation of existing lands. Generally speaking, the county was divided into two parts — the northern fenland and the southern upland. Wheat, rye and barley were mainly produced on the better upland soil and, of course, saffron. This was also good pasture ground, the areas around Wisbech and Newmarket producing excellent cheese and butter and in this area enclosure and consolidation proceeded apace during the Napoleonic War.[27]

The real need for improvement was in the fenland area, distinguished by its ditches, channels and drains, and usually under water most of the winter time. Arthur Young described the Fens when he visited them in 1805 as 'in so dreary a state, that waste was the only appropriate term to be given as the whole appeared to be in manifest danger of inundation.'[28] Hence, the continual interest in, and publicity for, drainage schemes, such as the controversial project known as the Eau Brink Cut.[29] This was a plan designed for improving navigation on the Ouse between Cambridge and King's Lynn and featured prominently in the Cambridge press after 1793. Progressive schemes were usually opposed, and in W. Gooch's survey, a chapter entitled 'Obstacles to Improvement' consists of only two lines, which summarise these difficulties concisely:

> In the uplands the expenses of enclosures;
> In the Fens, clashing interests.[30]

Generally speaking, Cambridge's fortunes in agriculture followed those of the rest of the country — enclosure and prosperity for the gentlemen farmers during the Napoleonic Wars, and depression after 1815. Then there were disturbances and riots in the county, notably the Littleport and Ely riots of 1816 and the agricultural labourers' revolt in 1830.[31] Not until the accession of Queen Victoria did the tide turn.

II

The want of elegance in the town and its lack of industry were more than amply compensated for, according to a contemporary guide book, "by the fine and interesting appearance of the University, whose noble buildings nearly encircled those of the town, justifying the remark of Fuller, that 'Oxford is a University in a town; but Cambridge a town in a University."[32] The University was then, and is now, a collection of colleges dominated by the imposing majesty of King's College Chapel with its lofty pinnacles and walls of buttressed stone. The colleges on one line, southwards, from red-bricked Magdalene, St. John's and Trinity, and on another through the town centre past Sidney Sussex, Christ's and Emmanuel, presented a complex of secluded greens, courts and cloisters, full of architectural beauty and all evolving in the town's midst. To many, Cambridge in the early nineteenth century was still basically the splendid survival of a mediaeval university with a small market town adjoining.

The same guide book informs us that 'very little business of any kind is carried on in Cambridge, but what is immediately or remotely connected with the University.'[33] As a centre of education it not only encouraged the need for bookbinding, printing and paper-making, it also stimulated town trade, building, lodging-houses and inns. The University had its ancient rights over certain aspects of town social and economic life: the examination and selling of all weights and measures, the destruction of unwholesome provisions found on sale in the market, the right to license alehouses, arrest and punish prostitutes, and also jurisdiction over undergraduates even when they had infringed town laws.[34] Owing to the nature of these rights the University was naturally unpopular both with town tradesmen and with the Corporation. Credit was usually allowed to undergraduates by townspeople, and because of non-payment of debts this often led to rioting and disorder.[35] Not all the blame lay with the town, though it challenged University rights at every opportunity. The University for its part clung tenaciously to these rights and many of the undergraduates, being rich, idle young men, were only happy when making a nuisance of themselves.[36] Their amusements were curious and assorted: billiards in Chesterton Village, boating to Grantchester, fights with bargees, wine parties of gargantuan dimensions, horse racing at Newmarket and, of course, rioting in the town.[37] Gunning stated that intoxication was 'the besetting sin of the University' and heavy drinking was common.[38] He also stated that the undergraduates he encountered 'in our dark streets were scarcely less ferocious than the members of the Mohock and Sweating Clubs.' Relations between Town and Gown got no better in the first decades of the nineteenth century, but the dependence of the town on the trade brought by the University gave the latter the upper hand in all disputes.

If many of the undergraduates appeared to do very little work, many of their tutors often did less, and the general tone of social life was low.[39] Subservient to Elizabethan statutes and the Anglican faith, senior members led their lives as churchmen and sportsmen, eccentrics and pedants. Many of them preserved in a remarkable way that intemperance of learning and diet inherited from the previous century. Scandals were common and well recorded by annalists such as Gunning. The University in the late eighteenth century has been accused of 'violating its statutes, misusing its endowments and neglecting its obligations', and no less an authority than Winstanley admits that 'it is impossible to dispute the substantial justice of this verdict.'[40] Also, throughout the eighteenth century the number of undergraduates continued to be low, and of these the numbers taking B.A. degrees nearly halved during the century, maintaining an average of only about 114 a year prior to 1800.[41]

The University was intimately connected with the political world, for the academic and parliamentary worlds worked closely together. Most of the dons wished to be on the winning side in politics, for on this depended preferment. The Duke of Newcastle had promoted Whig interests there until his death in 1768, but the political sympathies of the University were, in general, Tory. After the outbreak of the French Revolution the Whig party was very low in numbers and credit, and 'from this time those who professed themselves Whigs for the sake of what they could get, saw immediately that the cause was unprofitable and hopeless; and in a very short time scarcely a Whig was to be found among the resident members of the University.'[42] The chief representative of Tory interests in the University during the period was Isaac Milner, President of

Queens'. Gunning felt that Milner was determined to magnify the danger of Jacobinism in the University at the time, especially over the case of William Frend (Unitarian and Fellow of Jesus College). He was prosecuted before Milner himself for publishing a pamphlet entitled *Peace and Union,*[43] which was alleged to be an attack on the public religion. The Jesus Unitarians were seen as a threat by Milner, while Henry Gunning and Samuel Taylor Coleridge were both passionate partisans of Frend and defended his conduct.[44] However, he was tried, condemned and sentenced to be banished from the University, and later courts confirmed the decision. Gunning insisted that the prosecution was political rather than religious. The undergraduates were also unanimously in favour of Frend and refused to accept that he was a revolutionary and publisher of sedition. Gunning believed that he had himself been stamped as 'disaffected' by Milner's circle, and that this suspicion deprived a friend of his, Francis Wrangham, of a Fellowship at Trinity Hall.[45] The activities of people such as Frend, Gunning and Coleridge in the University must have caused some concern to the authorities. Although the war brought a tide of reaction against liberal principles, Gunning was one of a group of liberal gentlemen who asked Benjamin Flower, the printer, to come to Cambridge and set up a newspaper there,[46] and once it was established Samuel Taylor Coleridge used the paper to publish some of his poetry and advertise other literary works.[47] Meanwhile the anti-slavery movement in the University continued to be supported, but Catholic emancipation, the repeal of the Test and Corporation Acts and other popular liberal causes were opposed by the Senate.[48]

The students founded the Union in 1815 and the more serious-minded met to debate political and other questions in the room in Falcon Yard, behind the Red Lion in Petty Cury. The political outlook of the Union was that of intellectual liberalism, which in the repressive years after 1815 was often mistaken, especially by the Heads of Colleges, for English Jacobinism. The Union voted against the suspension of *Habeas Corpus,* and as a result was itself suspended. and remained silent for the next four years. Catholic emancipation, the key political issue in the 1820s, was repeatedly debated at the Union, and it was usually carried by small majorities before packed houses.[49] So the University, judging by the activities of dons and undergraduates, showed no lack of interest in the political issues of the period.

III

The distinction of producing the first English provincial newspaper belongs to East Anglia. This was *The Norwich Post* founded in 1701.[50] By the end of the century almost one hundred such newspapers were in existence, all of them being weekly editions.[51] The earliest Cambridge newspaper was *The Cambridge Journal and Weekly Flying Post* which appeared in 1744.[52] In a town in which the proportion of literacy must have been considerably higher than that of most country towns of the period, it may seem surprising that Cambridge was so slow in founding its first newspaper. Stamford, Northampton and Ipswich all had newspapers before 1720, Norwich having produced another four by the same date.[53] However, this usually merely indicated that a printer in the town was ambitious enough to risk his capital in such a venture and gamble on public interest and demand. It was neither an indication of a town's importance nor a reflection of the standard of literacy there.[54] In 1744 two keen London printers, Robert Walker and Thomas James, decided that there was a market for a weekly print in Cambridge. Walker was one of the first printers to recognize the existence and commercial possibilities of the new provincial reading public and had interests in many newspapers in different parts of the country.[55] Like all the provincial papers of the period the newspaper was local in name only, being compiled in the 'scissors and paste' tradition mainly from the London press.

It declared that it was neutral in politics, though in fact its sympathies were Tory, and proved moderately successful, being circulated in most of the adjoining counties.[56] Foreign affairs, diplomacy and war filled its pages in times of crisis, whereas in peacetime the content consisted mainly of detailed descriptions of trials, public executions and other matters of popular interest. Local news was confined to births, obituaries, crimes, accidents and 'unusual occurrences', and there was no editorial comment. In an effort to increase circulation the printers gave away weekly instalments of books: *The History of the Life and Reign of Queen Anne* in 1744, *The Life and Adventures of Simon, Lord Lovat* in 1746, but as the years passed the paper apparently became less and less adventurous, failing to exploit its favourable position with regard to the University, and not surprisingly, by 1762 a rival had appeared and five years later it had taken over the *Journal*.[57]

The first edition of *The Cambridge Chronicle* appeared on Saturday 30 October 1762, price 2½d., 'printed by T. Fletcher and F. Hodson at the New Printing Office on Market Hill.'[58] The new paper was well edited and from the outset endeavoured to cater for the University by inserting a section on the arts, reviewing books and stage productions, in addition to publishing University information of a general kind. Sarah James, who had taken over the *Journal* on the death of her husband in 1758 (Walker having severed his connection with the paper in 1753) continued to print in Trinity Street near the Theatre Coffee House, but eventually found the competition too keen and retired in 1766.[59] She informed her customers that because of her ill-health and 'a valuable consideration' having been offered by her rival editors she had decided to sell the *Journal* together with her whole stock of 'Printing Materials, Stationery and Public Medicines.'[60] The following week the first edition of *The Cambridge Chronicle and Journal* appeared.[61] By 1778 the name of Francis Hodson appeared alone as printer, and by his sons Edward and James the name of Hodson was associated with the paper for the next seventy years.

In choosing Cambridge as the town in which to found his newspaper Hodson must have been aware of the gamble he was taking. Initial expenses tended to be heavy (it cost £1,000 to set up *The Manchester Guardian* in 1821[62] and the risks were far greater in the provinces than in London, where a multitude of printers were ready to print for a few months and thereby give the proprietor a trial run and an estimate of sales.[63] In a country town premises had to be found, capital equipment bought, agents, carriers and distributors appointed and

THE
Cambridge CHRONICLE and JOURNAL.

PRINTED and PUBLISHED by FRANCIS HODSON, at the Corner of Green-Street, CAMBRIDGE.

Price SIX-PENCE.]   SATURDAY, SEPTEMBER 11, 1802.   NUMBER 1081.

LONDON.

goodwill gained, otherwise advertisements and public patronage might not result and without these there could be no newspaper.[64] The town already possessed one newspaper and its position on the main post road, plus its proximity to London, gave its inhabitants easy access to the more famous London prints. On the other hand the university town had obvious attractions both as a specialized market to cater for, regarding such items as news of Fellowships, preferments, elections, etc., and as a source of contributions such as essays, poems and letters. For his own part Hodson did his utmost to develop the section on local news and gossip and by the turn of the century his newspaper was firmly established, being popular in the town and also, apparently, 'handed about the University.'[65]

Hodson was first and foremost a printer; journalism was not his strong point, and indeed his newspaper followed the traditional eighteenth and early nineteenth-century pattern of provincial prints and had few pretensions. It measured about 13 x 20 in. and consisted of two leaves, four sides with five columns to a side. There were no headlines, sections simply being headed 'Sunday and Tuesday's Post', 'Foreign Affairs', 'Ship News', and so on. The first two sides were usually devoted to London news, advertisements and letters from the public. The third side dealt with local news, usually one or two columns, and was mainly concerned with births, deaths and marriages, local events and gossip. Advertisements and announcements usually filled in the remainder of this side. The final side was often a problem and at first tended to be filled with accounts of trials, extracts from books and often some poetry, but later House of Lords and House of Commons reports tended to fill this page, accompanied by the more literary advertisements. In many respects therefore the early *Cambridge Chronicle and Journal* was little more than a local advertising sheet. News continued to be 'lifted' from the London prints and until the 1830s the *Chronicle*, for example, had no editorial comment. This is not surprising because at that time there were few editors capable of writing leading articles. The majority were printers like Hodson, with no journalistic experience other than the 'scissors and paste' process of putting newspapers together. Nor were headlines usual or expected at the time. The provincial reader having waited seven days for his paper, was ready to read all the news.

The freshness of the printer's newspaper intelligence depended on many time-consuming operations. First of all the news had to be gathered from various sources and once received had to be set up in type, which at this time was still being done by hand. The compositor averaged about 1500 to 2000 ens of type per hour. The printing machine, up to about 1800, was just a fairly rudimentary wooden hand press. In the hand press the type forme was laid on a flat bed and an impression given by a hand-operated platen after the forme had been inked. The paper, which was cut in single sheets, had to be put on and taken off the press by hand, and was printed on one side only. The other side was printed on later, after the first side had dried. These wooden presses gave a relatively weak impression which was often smudged.[66] With two men operating it only two hundred impressions an hour of a single side could be produced.[67] Lord Stanhope's iron press replaced most of the wooden presses after 1800 giving a stronger and more accurate impression, but it did not increase the rate of output. Koenig in 1811 invented a steam-driven cylinder printing machine which could produce over 1,000 impressions per hour and by 1814 it was in production for *The Times*. By the 1840s modifications and improvements meant it was capable of producing almost 4,000 impressions per hour. Richard Hoe's short-feed rotary machine, capable of producing four times that many impressions per hour, was not introduced into England until the 1850s.[68] Provincial newspapers could hardly afford to keep in step with these technical changes because of the capital expense involved, but *The Manchester Guardian* had a Koenig press by 1828[69] and modest improvements, with about a twenty-year time-lag, tended to be the norm for the provincial weeklies.[70]

Throughout most of this period, therefore, provincial printing was slow, cumbrous and exacting[71] and the average printing office, such as Hodson's at the corner of Green Street, housing such simple traditional equipment, was a very small affair where no more than three or four compositors and pressmen would be employed. The master printer himself generally worked in the trade and would be satisfied with an output of 700 copies a week, which would be judged a respectable number by the standards of the time.[72] Compositors, though hard worked, were comparatively well paid, more so in Cambridge and Oxford than in other provincial towns because of the presence of the university printing offices, where more skilled compositors were required.[73]

The techniques of printing were probably the least of the problems with which Hodson was confronted. Distributing papers, collecting debts and acquiring advertisements were equally exacting and demanded stamina, enterprise and considerable organizing ability. Most printers, and Hodson is no exception, were extremely reticent on the subject of circulation, but from a study of the place of origin of advertisements in 1803 it would appear that the *Chronicle's* real influence lay in Cambridgeshire and Huntingdonshire and to a lesser degree in Northamptonshire, Bedfordshire and Hertfordshire. It was not successful in encroaching on the territory of the other local prints such as *The Norwich Mercury*, *The Ipswich Journal* and *The Suffolk Chronicle*.[74] Most of the *Chronicle's* success in its own area was largely due to the editor's ability to capture advertising revenue, the newspaper printing approximately eighty to a hundred advertisements per week over the whole period. Property sales, insurance, medicines, books and local announcements were the most general and they throw a vivid light on the state of society at the time. The income from advertisements was usually vital if the newspaper was to survive.[75] The problem of survival was made even more difficult by the 'taxes on knowledge' which reached their highest level between 1815 and 1836; every newspaper had to bear a government stamp and to pay a further tax on its advertisements.[76] Such expenses made it impossible to publish daily newspapers in the provinces, and no successful daily newspaper appeared outside London until the stamp duty was finally repealed in 1855.

In the early period then, up to 1760, G.A. Cranfield sees the development of the provincial, and the Cambridge, press in terms of a successful struggle against powerful odds: tiny profit margins, difficulties in production and distribution, the stamp taxes and metropolitan competition.[77] No country printer made any claim to originality or accepted responsibility for what he printed. The major part of these early weeklies was given to international events and especially to wars. Anything else was treated with scant respect, and domestic affairs in particular were almost completely ignored. By the 1780s information on parliamentary debates had some reader interest but comment on the fundamental issues of the day was studiously avoided. Printers tried not to take sides in local politics and this absence of commitment affected correspondence as well as news columns. In Cambridge for example, there was no discussion on the building of the important Denver Sluice in the Fens and no comment on the uproar over the new University regulations proposed by the Chancellor in 1750.[78] The primary importance of the early Cambridge press, therefore, was in its ability to communicate information. However, it is the role of the political advocate that is usually associated with the early nineteenth-century newspaper and when competitive situations multiplied, as a response to the need for a local medium of persuasion, newspapers became far more interesting. During the years 1780-1850 the press grew rapidly in power and influence and there followed a shift from non-local to local news in the provincial weekly. Rival newspapers encouraged and represented differing opinions in local communities while editorials and letters began to assume increasing importance as they opposed and defended contemporary political and social ideas. Though Cambridge remained a non-industrial university town, to a great extent it shared the challenges and problems posed by the growth of this new society. By the 1840s both the Tory and the Liberal newspapers in Cambridge were guiding and reflecting public opinion on a variety of contentious issues from poverty and railways to political corruption and the Corn Laws.

With the abolition of the newspaper stamp tax in the 1850s we enter a completely new period dominated by the 'Penny Daily' in London and to a lesser extent in the provinces — the beginnings, in fact, of the 'popular press.' With the *Daily Telegraph* selling 150,000 copies at a penny, a serious threat was posed to the traditional means of influencing attitudes and opinions in English society. Though dominated by the 'taxes on knowledge' the newspaper had developed from a primitive organisation, the by-product of a small printer's shop, into a highly complex and extraordinarily expensive business which affected the whole economy.[79]

NOTES AND REFERENCES

1   *Cantabrigia Depicta* (1781), pp. 7-8.
2   W. Wordsworth, *The Prelude*, III, ll.28-31.
3   A. Gray, *The Town of Cambridge: a history* (1925), p. 153.
4   T.D. Atkinson, *Cambridge Described and Illustrated* (1897), p. 130.

5   H. Gunning, *Reminiscences of the University, Town and County of Cambridge*, I, (1854), pp. 321-2.

6   C.H. Cooper, *Annals of Cambridge*, IV, (1845); *Cambridge Chronicle and Journal*, 22 June 1793, 26 May 1798, 4 April 1817, 1 Oct. 1824.

7   *A Description of the University, Town and County of Cambridgeshire* (1790), pp. 133-5.

8   Cooper, *Annals* IV, pp. 273, 331; Gray, *Town of Cambridge*, p. 185.

9   Cooper, *Annals* IV, pp. 432, 437.

10 F.A. Reeve, *Cambridge* (1964), p.98.

11 W. Gooch, *General View of the Agriculture of the County of Cambridge* (1813), p. 56.

12 Cooper, *Annals* IV, pp. 470, 637.

13 J.P.T. Bury, *J. Romilly's Cambridge Diary 1832-42: selected passages* (1967), p. x.

14 *A Description*, p. 120; Cooper, *Annals* III, (1842), p. 429; Reeve, *Cambridge*, p. 86.

15 Atkinson, *Cambridge Described*, p. 225.

16 *Victoria County History of Cambridgeshire and the Isle of Ely*, II, (1948), p. 103.

17 E.M. Hampson, *The Treatment of Poverty in Cambridgeshire 1597-1834* (1934), p. 106.

18 Gunning, *Reminiscences*, I, pp. 27-29.

19 D. Defoe, *A Tour thro' the whole island of Great Britain*, I, (1762), p. 89.

20 *New Cambridge Guide* (1830), p. 221.

21 E. Carter, *The History of the County of Cambridge* (1819), p. 13.

22 *A Description*, p. 120; D. and S. Lysons, *Magna Britannia*, II, (1808), p. 18.

23 *Cambridge Chronicle and Journal*, 12 Dec. 1795, 24 Mar., 2 June 1798.

24 Lysons & Lysons, *Magna Britannia*, II, p. 38.

25 Hampson, *Poverty in Cambs.* p. 216.

26 C. Vancouver, *General View of the Agriculture in the County of Cambridge* (1794), p. 193.

27 Carter, *History of Cambs.* pp. 4, 17.

28 A. Young, *Annals of Agriculture*, XLII, (1805), p. 539 et seq.

29 D. Summers, *The Great Ouse* (1973), Ch. 5.

30 Gooch, *General View of Agriculture*, Ch. XVI.

31 A.J. Peacock, *Bread or blood: a study of the agrarian riots in East Anglia in 1816* (1965); E.J. Hobsbawm and G. Rudé, *Captain Swing* (1969); *Cambridge Chronicle and Journal* 21, 28 June, 5 July 1816.

32 Quoted in *New Cambridge Guide* (1830), p. 222.

33 *Ibid.* p. 220.

34 D.A. Winstanley, *Unreformed Cambridge: a study of certain aspects of the University in the eighteenth century* (1935), pp. 23-32, 122-23, 212-17.

35 D.A. Winstanley, *Early Victorian Cambridge* (1940), pp. 126-27.

36 *Ibid.* pp. 209, 217-18.

37 P. Cradock, *The Cambridge Union* (1935), p. 5. See also O. Teichman, *The Cambridge undergraduate 100 years ago* (1926).

38 Gunning, *Reminiscences* I, p. 322; Teichman *op.cit.*, pp. 2, 7, 8; G. Pryme, *Autobiographic Recollections* (1870), p. 49.

39 Winstanley, *Unreformed Cambridge*, pp. 179-81.

40 *Ibid.* p. 1.
41 J.B. Mullinger, *A history of the University of Cambridge* (1888), p. 212.
42 Gunning, *Reminiscences* I, p. 189.
43 W. Frend, *Peace and Union Recommended* (1793).
44 A. Gray and F. Brittain, *A history of Jesus College Cambridge* (1960), p.124.
45 Gunning, *Reminiscences* I, pp. 299, 303, 326; II, 31-32.
46 B. Flower, *Statement of the Facts* (1808), p. XXIII.
47 See my 'Newspapers and Opinion in Cambridge 1780-1850', in *Transactions of the Cambridge Bibliographic Society* VI, (1971), p. 54.
48 Cooper, *Annals* IV, pp. 486, 507, 517, 551.
49 Cradock, *Cambridge Union*, pp. 3, 9, 21; Pryme, *Recollections*, pp. 117-18.
50 W.H. Allnutt, 'English Provincial Presses III', in *Bibliographica*, II (1896), pp. 276-308; G.A. Cranfield, *The Development of the Provincial Newspaper 1700-1760*, (1962), pp. 13-14.
51 G. Merle, 'The Provincial Newspaper Press' in *Westminster Review*, XII (1830), pp. 71, 94-98. For lists of provincial newspapers in the eighteenth and early nineteenth centuries see: G.A. Cranfield, 'A Handlist of English Provincial Newspapers and Periodicals 1700-1760', *Cambridge Bibliographical Society Monograph No. 2* (1952), also additions and corrections to this list in the *Transactions of the Cambridge Bibliographical Society*, II (1956), pp. 269-74; G. Watson's two sections in *The New Cambridge Bibliography of English Literature* (1971), II pp. 1353-69, III, 1794-1803 and *The Times Tercentenary Handlist of English and Welsh Newspapers* (1920), part II.
52 R. Bowes, 'On the First and Other Cambridge Newspapers', in *Proceedings of the Cambridge Antiquarian Society*, VIII (1895), p. 347.
53 *Ibid.* pp. 347-48.
54 G.A. Cranfield, 'The First Cambridge Newspaper', in *Proceedings of the Cambridge Antiquarian Society* (hereafter abbreviated to *P.C.A.S.*), XLV (1952), p. 5.
55 See A. Aspinall, 'Statistical Accounts of London Newspapers during the Eighteenth-Century', in *English Historical Review*, LXIII (1948).
56 Bowes, 'First Cambridge Newspapers', p. 351.
57 *Ibid.* pp. 350, 354.
58 *Cambridge Chronicle*, 30 Oct. 1762.
59 *Cambridge Journal and Weekly Flying Post*, 27 Dec. 1766.
60 *Ibid.* 27 Dec. 1766.
61 *The Cambridge Chronicle and Journal*, 3 Jan. 1767 (hereafter referred to as *Cambridge Chronicle* and abbreviated to *Camb. Chron.*)
62 A.E. Musson, 'Newspaper Printing in the Industrial Revolution', in *Economic History Review*, Ser. 2, X (1957-8), p. 413.
63 Merle, 'Provincial Press', pp. 70, 74.
64 *Camb. Chron.* 5 Jan. 1805.
65 *Ibid.* 5 Mar. 1802.
66 Contemporary accounts of printing processes and descriptions of printing techniques and technical changes are to be found in: T.Ford, *The Compositor's Handbook* (1854); C. Knight, *The Old Printer and the Modern Press* (1854); J. Moxon, *Mechanick Exercises on the Whole Art of Printing*, ed. H. Davis and H. Carter (1962); C.F. Partington, *The*

Printer's Complete Guide (1825); C.H. Timperley, *The Printer's Manual* (1838).

67 Musson, 'Newspaper Printing', p. 413.

68 *Ibid.* pp. 414-15.

69 *Ibid.* p. 418.

70 *Camb. Chron.*, 5 Jan. 1789; *Cambridge Intelligencer,* 5 July 1800.

71 See *Camb. Chron.* 26 April 1811, for a poem entitled 'Epitaph on a Compositor'.

72 Merle, 'Provincial Press', p. 79.

73 E. Howe, *The London Compositor* (1947), p. 253. See also S.C. Roberts, *The Evolution of Cambridge Publishing* (1956), for a survey of the development of the Cambridge University Press.

74 Cambridge University Library holds files of the *Norwich Mercury* 1749-1841 (imperfect), and of the *Ipswich Journal* 1760-1815 (very imperfect).

75 *Cambridge Intelligencer,* 18 June 1803; I. Asquith 'Advertising and the Press in the late eighteenth and early nineteenth centuries' in *Historical Journal* XVIII (1975), pp. 703-24.

76 C.D. Collet, *History of the Taxes on Knowledge,* I, (1899), p. 8. See also P. Hollis, *The Pauper Press* (1970), and *Appendix B.*

77 Cranfield, *Provincial Newspaper 1700-1760;* 'First Cambridge Newspaper' in *P.C.A.S.* XLV, 1952; R.M. Wiles, *Freshest Advices: Early Provincial Newspapers in England* (1965), p.25.

78 *Cambridge Journal,* 31 Oct., 7, 28 Nov., Dec. 1747; Cranfield, *Provincial Newspaper,* p.86.

79 See A.P. Wadsworth, 'Newspaper Circulations 1800-1954,' in *Transactions of the Manchester Statistical Society,* 1954-55; H.A. Innis, 'The Newspaper in Economic Development' in *Journal of Economic History. Supplement* Dec. 1942.

2
Politics, War and Opinion 1790-1815

I

From 1789 to 1815 events outside England dominated the domestic political scene. English reaction to the French Revolution has been well described – dissenters and radicals, poets and intellectuals welcomed what appeared to them to be the dawn of a new era in European history.[1] Corresponding clubs and societies were founded in London, Norwich, Sheffield and elsewhere and inspired by events across the Channel and the writings of Tom Paine, their members renewed the constitutional agitation of the 1780s for the reform of Parliament.[2] By 1792 the Sheffield Constitutional Society backed by Joseph Gales, the Unitarian printer, could muster thousands of members to celebrate French victories and demand universal suffrage.[3] Norwich rivalled Sheffield as a centre of English Jacobinism and displaying such energy and enthusiasm these new societies, it appeared, would revitalise the whole of English politics.[4]

However, they were minority societies, and subsequent events in France rapidly turned popular feeling against them. Loyalist Associations were founded in every major city and town and soon Church-and-King mobs hounded radicals and denounced Jacobins. Pitt's government prosecuted reformers, increased the stamp duty on newspapers and in the years that followed the outbreak of war with France regarded every newspaper editor as 'the raw material of a traitor.'[5] Though it may be difficult to determine how far the Association movement was spontaneous, conformist or merely mercenary, it achieved the desired result. Radicalism was severely checked and public expression of dissent was repressed.[6] In Cambridge the French Revolution brought with it the suppression of reforming societies; their meetings were held less frequently and many members deserted. There were suspicions of Jacobinism in the University and demonstrations of loyalty in the town. In 1793 over one hundred publicans agreed to inform the magistrates of seditious activities and an effigy of Paine was paraded through the streets and ceremonially burnt on Market Hill 'amidst the loyal acclamations of surrounding hundreds.'[7]

The year 1793 was the beginning of a highly significant period in the history of English journalism. The war with France placed an unprecedented emphasis upon newspapers as organs of public opinion and information.[8] Though Hodson's sympathies were Tory it is difficult at first to discover direct evidence of this fact in the pages of the *Chronicle*. His aim was to print a local paper to be read by Whig and Tory alike, as the adoption of a firm party line would merely estrange potential customers. Influenced, no doubt, by the widespread manifestations of loyalty in the town after 1793 he openly declared his support for the war effort and the Prime Minster, Pitt.[9] Despite the unpropitiousness of the times there remained in Cambridge a few liberals sufficiently enterprising to launch a new Cambridge newspaper – *The Cambridge Intelligencer.* Among them was a Hertfordshire farmer, brewer and staunch liberal, Richard Flower, who persuaded his elder brother Benjamin to become editor.[10]

Though the *Intelligencer* was to achieve national recognition as a provincial journal, remarkably little is known about Benjamin Flower. His career in journalism poses almost as many questions as it answers. However he does emerge as a radical figure of importance, one who helped to ensure that liberal ideas continued to be discussed during this critical and intensely repressive period of English history.[11] He was born in London in 1755.[12] His father was a successful city businessman and built up a profitable trading concern before his death in 1788. Benjamin and his brother William shared the inheritance but their subsequent partnership was not a success. It is clear that Benjamin did not inherit any of his father's ability in speculation, and he quickly lost his share of the business on the stock market. Disappointed and frustrated, he passed through a variety of occupations in trading, banking and education before travelling through Europe in the late 1780s as a commercial agent. His impression of events in France, where he witnessed some of the most interesting scenes of the French Revolution, inspired him to write a rather discursive work on the French constitution which attracted a large share of public attention.[13] Although he denounced the leadership of the Revolution, he maintained his admiration for the principles of the National Assembly. Approached by his brother Richard to undertake the establishment of a liberal weekly newspaper in Cambridge, Flower at first saw only the difficulties involved in such a venture, but he eventually accepted. The newly-founded *Cambridge Intelligencer* was to be no ordinary provincial print. At that time editorial comment was still rare in newspapers, and almost unknown in the provincial press.[14] While it is true that letters to the press were used for the expression of opinion, and protest meetings were advertised and sometimes reported, the pamphlet continued to be the popular medium for propagandists and reformers.[15] The London press remained dominant, and, even towards the end of the eighteenth century, according to the editor of *New Monthly Magazine,* 'there was not a single provincial editor who would have hazarded an original article on public affairs.'[16] Flower was to prove an exception. He set out to instruct public opinion by reporting parliamentary proceedings and political meetings, and, much more important, by criticising party and authority through powerfully-worded editorial articles. *The Intelligencer* was the first provincial newspaper in England to develop these new techniques and continue them for an appreciable length of time.[17]

Flower's father had been a prominent Dissenter, and Benjamin was greatly influenced by his religious background. The house was frequently used as a meeting place and discussion centre for other Dissenting ministers and evangelical friends.[18] The result was that Benjamin became a student of theology early in life, gradually developing the ardent love of religious liberty which characterised Dissenters. Eventually, his study of the sermons of the nonconformist Rev. Robert Robinson[19] of Cambridge cleared his mind of a number of religious uncertainties and confirmed his belief in Arianism, one of the less radical branches of English Unitarianism. The connection between newspapers and Dissent during this period, and particularly the contribution of Unitarians to the press, has received some attention.[20] Flower was not untypical among members of the sect in accepting a newspaper editorship. Besides Flower there were, for example, Gales of *The Sheffield Register*,[21] Taylor, Garnett and Harland of *The Manchester Guardian*, and Ward of *The Sheffield Independent*. They all displayed earnestness in religion, politics and business and, because they believed profoundly that the only sound basis of government was an educated public opinion, they found journalism extremely attractive. Flower acknowledged that he was a man with a mission, and had entered the world of political and religious controversy because he felt it 'his bounden duty.'[22] Further, like many Unitarians, he possessed what might be called 'a mentality of revolt', believing above all in the natural right to freedom of conscience — conscience which a man *must* obey — a spiritual duty which bade him stand up and be counted whatever the consequences: 'no events will turn us aside from the path of duty.'[23] Rejection of human authority, assertion of power in the congregation as opposed to the hierarchy, toleration, and freedom to criticise, were his main tenets. Flower was therefore very much a Rational Dissenter, a disciple in the tradition of Joseph Priestley and Richard Price.[24]

The impact of Dissenters on public opinion in the last decades of the eighteenth century was remarkable. They were great believers not only in the power of the press but also in that of association.[25] The Baptist Robert Robinson, for example, founded the Cambridge Constitutional Society, which distinguished itself in the county movement for parliamentary reform[26] and was also one of the first bodies to petition Parliament for the abolition of the slave trade.[27] The members of the society, who were chiefly townsmen and Dissenters, adopted in 1790 the fundamental principles of the Revolution Society, including the natural right of the individual to life, liberty and property, government by consent and parliamentary reform. Already the inheritors of the religious thought of Milton and Locke, they now embraced the more revolutionary political ideas of Paine — the rights of man and sovereignty of the people.[28] Both Robinson and Flower believed there was a special connection between religion and politics and were not afraid to introduce politics into their sermons in villages and barns around the county.[29]

Flower's *Intelligencer* became a sort of nation-wide congregational magazine for Rational Dissenters and included extracts, letters and articles from George Dyer, Mrs. Barbauld, Gilbert Wakefield, Christopher Wyvill, Henry Crabb Robinson and Mary Wollstonecraft.[30] It published some of the early poems of Coleridge[31] as well as providing a full record of dissenting activities and misfortunes during a period when Dissenters were singled out as special objects of attack. Their attempts to get religious freedom for those who dissented from the

Benjamin Flower

THE CAMBRIDGE INTELLIGENCER.

PRINTED and PUBLISHED by BENJAMIN FLOWER, Bridge-Street, CAMBRIDGE.

NUMBER 404.	SATURDAY, April 11, 1801.	Price Six-Pence.

Let it be imprinted upon your minds, let it be instilled into your children, that the Liberty of the Press is the PALLADIUM of all the civil, political and religious Rights of Freemen. JUNIUS.

This Paper is circulated through the Town and Villages in the Counties of CAMBRIDGE, HUNTINGDON, LINCOLN, RUTLAND, BEDFORD, and HERTFORD; likewise through a considerable Part of NORTHAMPTONSHIRE, LEICESTERSHIRE, NOTTINGHAMSHIRE, LANCASHIRE, YORKSHIRE, NORFOLK, SUFFOLK, ESSEX, KENT, and the Eastern and Northern Counties.—The circulation has likewise been considerably extended to LONDON, BRISTOL, OXFORD, PLYMOUTH, the Western Counties, and in WALES and SCOTLAND.—Any Person may have this Paper sent free of Postage, to any Post-Town of Great Britain, for SEVEN SHILLINGS a Quarter, FIFTEEN SHILLINGS the Half Year, or if the Money is paid in advance, FOURTEEN SHILLINGS the Half Year, or ONE POUND SIX SHILLINGS a Year; by sending a Letter, (Post Paid) to the Printer, where Subscriptions, Advertisements and authentic Articles of Intelligence are received. ADVERTISEMENTS are taken in by W. TAYLER, WARWICK-SQUARE, and at the CHAPTER COFFEE HOUSE, PATER-NOSTER-ROW; and ORDERS and ADVERTISEMENTS by T. CONDER, BUCKLERSBURY, LONDON, and by the Country Agents.

doctrines of the established Church aroused considerable indignation, while the rapid spread of Unitarian views, especially at Cambridge University, caused some alarm. A number of Dissenters tried for alleged sedition were clergymen who had left the Church to become Unitarians, the best known being Frend of Jesus College, Fyche Palmer of Queens' and Dr. Jebb of St. John's.[32] This tradition of religious and political dissent in Cambridge in the eighteenth century[33] probably explains why the town was chosen as the base from which to launch Flower's radical *Cambridge Intelligencer.*

Premises for Flower were found in Bridge Street, and the first issue of the *Intelligencer* appeared in July 1793. The format was similar to that of its rival, the Tory *Cambridge Chronicle,* and most other eighteenth-century newspapers. But the content was different, for the *Intelligencer* paraded an editorial — often running into four columns, usually denouncing the war with France or anything that savoured of abuse, corruption or oppression. The shortage of advertisements was noticeable, the average number hardly ever rising above ten per week in the early years, sixteen per week overall, compared to the eighty per week average of the rival *Chronicle.* The paper was never a commercial success. It earned Flower a mere one hundred and forty pounds per annum.[34] Paradoxically, the circulation of the paper continued to grow at an astonishing rate for a country print. Flower was justifiably proud of the figures and usually commented on them in the January editorial: 'At the commencement of the paper in July 1793, our number was six hundred and fifty; from that period to June 1797 it gradually increased to two thousand seven hundred. The act passed in July last, levying three halfpence additional duty on Newspapers, reduced our Circulation to eighteen hundred, since when it has been increasing, and our present number is nearly two thousand.'[35] This circulation, at a time when hundreds per week was regarded as satisfactory for a provincial print, was surprising.[36] One of the reasons why the *Intelligencer* displayed so few advertisements was that it was never merely a local newspaper.

A look at Flower's impressive distribution list on January 24 1801, for example, clearly illustrates that his paper was a national one. London and Middlesex took 250 papers and Scotland 100 while Yorkshire and the West Country were particularly well served with distribution agents. Dublin and the Isle of Man also received copies of the paper. Advertisements in that year came from as far afield as Bristol and Blackburn, Evesham and Leeds. Letters to the editor were received from every part of Great Britain during the newspaper's ten years of existence. Though the newspaper was apparently handed about the University, the disappointed editor considered his local circulation trifling and his advertisements scarcely worth mentioning.[37] It was some compensation to know that the *Intelligencer* was widely read in the north of England, especially in Liverpool, Sheffield, Leeds and Nottingham.[38] Flower complained on three occasions that some of his papers, bound for Scotland, had been damaged on the northern road.[39] The Town Clerk at Tiverton claimed that it was one of the radical papers that had much support in the area and commented that 'the industry used to procure the Jacobin papers is remarkable.'[40] John Guest, the founder of the Dowlais iron works, introduced it into his part of South Wales.[41]

Weston Hatfield, editor of *The Cambridge Independent Press* and Flower's radical successor in Cambridge, asserted that it was 'read, admired and hated from the town of Berwick-upon-Tweed to the Land's End in Cornwall.'[42] W.J. Fox the editor of the Unitarian *Monthly Repository* claimed it was read 'all over the country',[43] and the editor of the Tory *Anti-Jacobin* expressed surprise 'at its extensive circulation.'[44] Coleridge warmly recommended it as an alternative to his ill-fated periodical *The Watchman*.[45] It consoled Priestley in his American exile and even reached the transported Fyche Palmer at Botany Bay.[46] The significance of this is not so much that Flower achieved a relatively high circulation for the *Intelligencer,* by standards current at the time, but that he was publishing vigorous and controversial editorials designed to stimulate and influence opinion throughout England. Unlike his fellow provincial editors, he was not deterred from publishing by the severity of Pitt's repressive domestic policy. He ceased to be a parasite on the London press and discarded the 'scissors and paste' tradition. This was something entirely new in provincial journalism.

II

During the 1790s Flower used the editorial columns of the *Intelligencer* to condemn and oppose the Napoleonic War. He questioned government motives for participating in the war and insisted that it was not only unchristian and unjustifiable but its economic effects would be disastrous. 'We are engaged', he wrote, 'in a Quixotic war which threatens to ruin our manufacturers, and in which our best blood and treasures are daily expending under the pretence of prosecuting the spread of Jacobin principles.'[47] He resisted the prevailing tendency to condemn France: 'The fact is we are as wicked in most respects, and wickeder in some, than the French.'[48] Letters soon began to arrive from all over England denouncing the war and echoing Flower's sentiments.[49] In his opinion, Pitt was the minister most responsible for the continued evils of the war. Consequently he vigorously attacked every war-time budget, lamenting in 1797:

> In the unsuccessful prosecution of this war of frenzy and wickedness, our ministers have added *TWO HUNDRED MILLIONS* to our debt, and have entailed perpetual taxes to the amount of *EIGHT MILLIONS;* they have at the same time wounded our Constitution in its most precious vitals, and robbed us of some of our best birth-right privileges; they have, in short, done everything in their power to corrupt, impoverish, enslave and ruin us at home, and to render us contemptible abroad; they have deluged Europe with blood and after being foiled in every respect . . . such Ministers should be driven from their places, and be brought to the bar of their country to answer for their numberless crimes. This . . . is our most *IMPERIOUS DUTY*.[50]

He also blamed the war for the high price of bread and provisions, maintaining in another of his comprehensive editorial attacks that the much maligned farmers had already received too much blame for a situation not of their making and out of which others profited more substantially and more unjustly.[51] Flower was careful to keep the people of Cambridge informed as to how their representatives in Parliament voted on this vitally important issue. Unfortunately, in Flower's eyes, it was usually in favour of the war.

To be **SOLD** by **PRIVATE CONTRACT.**

ELEVEN ACRES of **ARABLE LAND** in high cultivation in the Parish of *Burrell*, CAMBRIDGESHIRE, in the occupation of Mr. BRIDGE-MAN who is tenant at will.

For further particulars enquire of Mr. B. RYDER, Henham, Eflex.

TO ADVERTISERS IN GENERAL.

CAMBRIDGE INTELLIGENCER.

Published every Saturday.

NUMBER CIRCULATED—1800.

The following are the principal places.
CAMBRIDGE, ELY, and the adjacent TOWNS and
VILLAGES.

LONDON and MIDDLESEX, (250 Papers)
EDINBURGH, GLASGOW, ABERDEEN, &c.

(100 Papers.)

BEDS—Bedford, Afpley, Woburn, Luton, Big-glefwade, Dunftable, Ampthill, Leighton-Buzzard.

BUCKS—High Wycombe, Chefham, Beaconsfield, Olney, Aylefbury, Amerfham, Eton, Great-Marlow, Gold Hill, Newport Pagnell.

BERKS.—Maidenhead, Abingdon, Wantage, Farring-don, Reading, Hungerford, Windfor, New-bury.

CORNWALL—Helfton, Grampound, St. Auftell, Penryn, Callington, Bodmin, Redruth, Launcefton, Falmouth.

CUMBERLAND—Penrith, Thrunfby.

CHESHIRE.—Chefter.

DORSET.—Dorchefter, Sherbourne, Blandford, Wareham, Cerne Abbas, Poole, Bridport,

DEVON.—Exeter, Tiverton, Plymouth, Torring-ton, Star Crofs, Afhburton, Topfham, Plymouth Dock, Axminfter, Collump-ton, North Tawton, Taviftock, Exmouth, Kingfbridge, Dudbrook, Stonehoufe, More-ton-Hampftead, Bow, Arpford, Ottery, Honiton, Brixham.

DERBYSH.—Derby, Broadholme, Afhburn, Mat-lock, Mayfield, Bonfall, Cromford, Bake-well, Wirkfworth, Belpar.

DURHAM.—Durham, Darlington, Bifhop-Middle-ham, Barnard-Caftle.

ESSEX.—Chelmsford, Bocking, Colchefter, Bille-ricay, Braintree, Stebbing, Dunmow, Sible-Hedingham, Finchingfield, Witham, Ongar, Weathersfield, Langford, Malden, Little Wathern, Dedham, Kelveden, Halftead, Bifhop Stortford, Saffron Walden, Thax-tead, Harlow, Coggefhall.

GLOUCESTER.—Gloucefter, Nailfworth, Tewkes-bury, Cirencefter, Bourton on the Water, Chipping Sodbury, Terbury, Stow on the Wold, Thornbury, Kingfton, Wotton un-der Edge, Newnham, Cambden, Stroud, Cheltenham, Chalford Hill, Hampton, Winchcomb, Northleach, Newent, Blake-ney.

HERTS.—Hertford, Rickmanfworth, Royfton, Bal-dock, Gt. Berkhampftead, King's Lang-ley, St. Albans, Hitchin, Sawbridgeworth, Stevenage, Welwyn, Hemel Hempftead, Buntingford, Ware.

HEREFORD.—Hereford, Stoke Edyth, Leominfter, Rofs.

HUNTS.—Huntingdon, St. Ives, Somerfham, Ram-fey, St. Ives, Kimbolton, Paxton, Staughton way, Bluntifham, Stilton, Yaxley.

HAMPSHIRE, &c.—Newport, (Ifle of Wight), Ports-mouth, Gofport, Whitchurch, Overton, Andover, Portfea, Havant, Fareham.

KENT.—Canterbury, Rochefter, Hawkhurft, Farn-ingham, Chatham, Feverfham, Maidftone, Seven Oaks, Tenterden, Sheernefs, Dept-ford, Afhford, Cranbrook, Ticchurft, Tun-bridge Wells, Aylesford, Eaft Malling, Sutton, Weft Malling, Folkftone, Deal, Gravefend.

LEICESTER.—Leicefter, Afhby de la Zouch, Lough-borough, Hinkley, Coftock, Melton Mow-bray, Market Harborough, Lutterworth.

LANCASH.—Lancafter, Blackburn, Liverpool, Colne, Prefton, Wigan, Garftang, Bolton, Man-chefter.

LINCOLNSHIRE.—Lincoln, Louth, Grantham, Bof-ton, Spalding, Spilfby, Wragby, Stam-ford, Barton, Gainfborough, Kirton Lind-fey, Market Deeping, Barton on Humber, Horncaftle, Alford, Donnington, Buck-minfter, Swinfted.

NORTHAMPT.—Northampton, Long Buckby, Wels-ford, Towcefter, Daventry, Kettering, Oundle, Wellingborough, Higham Ferrars, Thrapftone, Brigftock, Peterborough.

NOTTS.—Nottingham, Mansfield, Sutton, Tuxford, Bingham, Retford, Workfop, Newark.

NORFOLK.—Norwich, Yarmouth, Thetford, Dere-ham, Burnham Market, Swaffham, Wy-mondham, Melton Conftable, Fakenham, Kempton, Tofts, Rainham, Lynn, Down-ham, Attleburgh.

NORTHUMBERLAND.—Newcaftle, Morpeth.

OXON.—Oxford, Burford, Charlbury, Woodftock, Banbury, Bampton, Witney, Hook Norton, Chipping Norton.

RUTLAND.—Oakham, Uppingham.

STAFFORDS.—Bilftone, Wolverhampton, Stoke upon Trent, Newcaftle, Litchfield.

SHROPSHIRE.—Shrewfbury, Ludlow, Wellington.

SUFFOLK.—Ipfwich, Sproughton, Sudbury, Yox-ford, Woodbridge, Lavenham, Mendle-fham, Stow Market, Hadleigh, Bury, Mildenhall, Loweftoff.

SURRY.—Guildford, Godalming, Streatham, Rich-mond, Mitcham, Chertfey.

SUSSEX.—Lewes, Ditchling, Billinghurft, Petworth, Rotherfield, Battle, Brighton, Cuckfield.

SOMERSET.—Taunton, Axminfter, South Petherton, Yeovil, Wivelifcombe, Crewkerne, Briftol, Frome, Bridgewater, Langport, Glafton-bury, Shipton Mallet, Martock, Bath.

WARWICK.—Warwick, Atherftone, Coventry, Nun-eaton, Alcefter, Aftwood, Birmingham, Bedworth.

WILTS.—Devizes, Great Bedwin, Warminfter, Mere, Bradford, Malmefbury.

WORCESTER.—Worcefter, Kidderminfter, Stour-bridge, Evefham, Broomfgrove, Bewdley, Redditch, Upton upon Severn, Perfhore, Droitwich.

WESTMORELAND.—Kendall, Appleby, Brough.

YORKSHIRE.—York, Beverley, Bridlington, Hull, Northallerton, Scarborough, Yarm, Drif-field, Knarefborough, Bingley, Rotherham, Bradford, Holmfirth, Ripon, Wakefield, Leeds, Skipton, Gretabridge, Bedale, Settle, Carlton, Gargrave, Skipton in Craven, Clifton, Keighley, Thorp Arch, Weatherby, Marfke, Richmond, Huddersfield, Hard-ing, Morley, Pudfey, Pocklington, Stock-ton on Tees, Sheffield, Pontefract, Pick-ering, Kippax, Ackworth, Otley.

WALES—Brecon.

CARDIGANSHIRE.—Caftlehowell, Lampeter, Pen-rhygaled.

CARMARTHEN.—Caermarthen, St. Cleaers, Lan-dovery.

GLAMORGAN.—Swanfea, CydCyr, Pendarrin, Neath, Merthier Tidwell, Cardiff, Cowbridge, Bridge End.

MONMOUTHSHIRE.—Monmouth, Landfaintfrood, Cheptlow, Ponty Pool, Newport.

PEMBROKESHIRE.—Narbeth, Tavernffpite. Haver-ford Weft.

CARNARVONSHIRE.—Anglefea, Rhydyelafridy.

BERWICK ON TWEED.—Ifle of Man.—Dublin.

Cambridge Intelligencer Distribution Agents

He found the Whig response disappointing: 'not one resolution was entered into by the [Whig] Club respecting either the necessity of Peace nor of a Reform of Parliament.'[52] Under the circumstances he could not feel very optimistic about the possibilities of peace: 'as long as the people . . . are silent and do not petition for peace, we make no doubt but ministers will say, that this war of slaughter and devastation is persevered in, with the full approbation of the public.'[53] Impartial political comment was therefore his duty as 'Most of the public prints are in general prostituted and servile.'[54] Only with Gales of the *Sheffield Register* did he feel in complete agreement and though he excepted from condemnation the *Morning Chronicle,* the *Morning Post* and the *London Courier,* all of which were capable of putting forward reformist and near radical ideas on occasion,[55] there were too many instances when other liberal prints like the *Leeds Mercury* (under Edward Baines), apostasised.[56] After ten years of war he was bitterly disillusioned at its resumption, following a two-year period of peace, in 1803:

> although we have good reason to believe the war is far from being popular;
> although we know that in some of our principal commercial cities (Manchester
> in particular), great discontent prevails on account of the stagnation of trade,
> the reduced wages and the want of employment of thousands of the manu-
> facturing classes – (some of the bitter fruits of the present war) – yet their
> execrations of the system though "deep" are so far from being loud that they
> are to the public scarcely audible . . . Lethargy benumbs the faculties of our
> countrymen and Fear, lest in case of opposition to the measures of ministers,
> the system of terror should be revived, together with some paltry, immediate
> self interest prevents the expression of the public voice. Not one remon-
> strance against the war, not one petition to the throne for a change of measures
> and for peaceable counsels appears to have been thought of.[57]

As a result of this type of editorial, Flower himself often came under attack from correspondents and on one occasion was charged with printing and pub-lishing 'seditious pamphlets calculated to inflame the minds of the lower class of people.'[58] Baines accused him of holding forth from 'his dictatorial throne and playing the part of the Tyrant in the cause of Freedom.'[59] A correspondent to the *Anti-Jacobin* informed its editor that *The Cambridge Intelligencer* was a paper 'which for its rancour and scurrility might do much mischief among the Yeomanry and Peasantry of the Northern Counties.' After briefly investigating the matter, the editor of the government-supported *Anti-Jacobin* found the newspaper 'infinitely more vile and detestable than we had been led to sur-mise' and expressed surprise at its lack of advertisements, its extensive circula-tion and the sentiments it expressed 'with the frankness of a Marat.'[60] Flower was not overawed by this and, after referring to the *Anti-Jacobin's* own circula-tion problems and complete absence of advertisements, concluded: 'we can ad-dress our present adversary in language similar to that of the Angel in Milton to his adversary Satan – I know thy strength and thou knowest mine!'[61]

However, Flower's friends became increasingly concerned for his safety and in 1796 Thomas Jones, the Bursar of Trinity College, wrote to William Frend, 'I am afraid lest Ben Flower's fiery indignation against the present measures should expose him to the penalties of one of the late bills. A hint will be of use to him . . .'[62] However, the 'hints', if given, were not sufficient to dissuade Flower from what he regarded as his religious duty. The editor of *The Cambridge Chronicle* on the other hand, in his very rare editorial comments, supported Pitt, his government and the waging of the war. According to Hodson, the blame for the war lay with France,[63] militia volunteers were to be encouraged, and the suspension of *Habeas Corpus* accepted as a wartime necessity.[64] Furthermore ministers deserved praise for the 'patience with which they bear the daily libels dictated by insolence, ignorance, imprudence and scurrility', and Pitt, because 'he has made the good of his country the invariable rule of his conduct.'[65] In general, Town and Gown stood fast for the government and the war effort. As a result, Dissenters were subjected to much annoyance and some violence. Flower himself once had his office windows smashed by a shower of stones from a Church-and-King mob.[66] Such disturbances were suppressed by the authorities, but with little sympathy for the victims.

It is difficult to be precise about Flower's attitude to C.J. Fox, the leader of the Whig opposition in the Commons. Flower insisted that he was not a party man: 'The politics of both these parties, we are sorry to say, are equally uninteresting to the public.'[67] He was only prepared to accept reformers 'in proportion to the purity of their ends.'[68] Despite these protestations he hoped for much from Fox (who apparently 'honoured him with his correspondence'),[69] and their reform opinions appear similar. Flower often praised Fox, the Whig Club and the Foxites for their exertions in Parliament on behalf of liberty and reform, and even recommended that a Whig Club be set up in Cambridge.[70] Disillusioned by public apathy, he advocated Whig secession from Parliament in 1795 and called for the resurrection of the aristocratic Society of the Friends of the People in 1797 because 'The people at large want an association of leading public men to whom they can look up with confidence.' When a disillusioned Fox finally seceded in the same year, Flower regretted that 'such abilities and integrity are lost to the country', but on the other hand the public because of 'their neglect and ingratitude do not deserve the exertions of these illustrious statesmen.'[71] On other occasions he was ready to criticise Fox and his followers, too many of them, in his opinion, being Whigs 'only in name.'[72]

His relationship with the radicals was also problematic. Though favoured with advertisements for the *Intelligencer* from the Society for Constitutional Information, the London Corresponding Society and the Sheffield Constitutional Society, he felt their demands were too extreme. He criticised, for example, the chairman of the Sheffield Reform Society, Henry Redhead Yorke, maintaining that he appeared 'a much more suitable President for the Jacobin Club or the Revolutionary Tribunal at Paris, than for a respectable society of English Reformers.'[73] There was too much of the republican in Yorke for his liking. Though agreeing in principle with the demand for annual parliaments, the secret ballot and universal suffrage, he stressed the danger of stubbornly insisting on these demands as the only radical solution. Their implementation might lead to even more bribery and corruption, and he was not yet convinced that the English people were 'fully prepared for the exercise of the enjoyment of the most abstract rights in the most unlimited degree.'[74] However, he denied that the Corresponding societies were revolutionary or subversive, and insisted on their right 'to peaceably call the attention of the public to the grand Business of Reform in general', though he did not entirely accept 'their speculative opinions on reform.'[75]

This approach did not go far enough for the radicals. Major Cartwright, for example, rejected such caution and was prepared to campaign vigorously for universal suffrage and a secret ballot.[76] He was cynical about the secession of Fox, a politician 'too much actuated by a party spirit', and insisted that he should have remained in the Commons and stayed active in defence of the constitution.[77] Flower believed that such an attitude was doctrinaire and liable to divide the reform movement. He condemned the radicals' apparent inability to ally with the Whigs and middle classes in an effort to secure 'a more equal and frequent representation.'[78] A united movement would have the merit of defining more sharply those who were for change and those who wished to preserve the status quo. In fact, there was a complete lack of co-ordination, and the moderates soon discovered how disagreeable it was to be moderate in a world running to extremes. Denounced by their own class as Jacobins they were simultaneously mocked by the radicals for being patronising, cautious and half-hearted. Disillusionment rapidly set in and soon animosities between fellow reformers seemed to resemble nothing more than the struggles of men fighting in a condemned cell.[79] As a result, even Flower was occasionally driven to favour extremism in the cause of liberty. When, for example, the Triumvirate overthrew the Directory of Paris in 1797 and instituted a military despotism, he urged the French 'to what is now their most sacred duty — INSURRECTION!'[80] Rebellion might also be deemed lawful in the case of the down-trodden peasants of Ireland and the oppressed and exploited slaves of the West Indies.[81]

However, on balance, it would appear that Flower's political philosophy was largely a product of the constitutionalism of the 1780s. Though an element of Painite radicalism occasionally emerges, he was basically a follower of Priestley, Price and Christopher Wyvill,[82] whom he praised for their independent principles and sincere attachment to the constitution.[83] He looked to the extension of the franchise rather than universal manhood suffrage to secure civil liberty, accepting as he did that 'the true spirit of liberty is a spirit of order . . . a strict observance of the laws and a peaceable conduct.'[84] If there were abuses or unjust laws, then Parliament could, and should, change them. For Flower, therefore, reform of Parliament was the key and so he gave full coverage to public meetings and petitions, local elections and parliamentary debates, hoping thereby to gain as wide an audience as possible and acquaint the public with the realities of political life. He never disguised his own sentiments on reform and took every available opportunity to preach them but, 'as every man must be a Jacobin who expresses a wish for reform', he was often forced simply to report events and to leave 'the subject to the reflection of our readers.'[85]

Pitt's government appeared content to suffer Flower and his radical opinions. An investigation of correspondence to and from the various departments of the Home Office,[86] during the period when Flower was active, reveals some letters concerning Joseph Gales ('the infamous Printer of the Sheffield Paper')[87] and the *Morning Post* ('the most impudent and seditious Paper which comes out')[88] but there is only one reference to *The Cambridge Intelligencer*. During a corn riot in Banbury in September 1800, one of the leaders, a certain Thomas Whitmore, from Middleton in Northamptonshire, was apprehended. He had in his possession a copy of *The Cambridge Intelligencer* and a letter referring to the benefits that had resulted from the recent riots at Nottingham.[89] These were described by another correspondent as 'papers the most virulent against government.'[90] The enclosed papers did not elicit a reply from the Duke of Portland, who was obviously much more interested in endeavouring to trace the many *anonymous* seditious papers being printed and distributed at the time. Lord Hardwicke, who was well aware of Flower and his radical editorials, appeared to share Portland's attitude. Commenting on the probability of Dissenters being involved in corn riots in the county, he assured the Home Office that 'those Dissenters who wished ill of the Government, did not wish ill to it in that sort of way.'[91] On the other hand, he accepted that Flower was 'the leading Dissenter' and major opponent of the government in town and county.[92] From more recent experience, Hardwicke had come to appreciate both the high standard of reporting and the propaganda value of the *Intelligencer*, so much so that when he learned of the probable closure of the Tory *Cambridge Chronicle* in 1802 he wrote to his half-brother, Charles Yorke, expressing the utmost concern that Hodson's *Chronicle* should not 'fall into bad hands . . . I will state the case to Addington . . . I think Hodson should be supported; but if he cannot his paper should be transferred to some loyal subjects . . . who will not only, with insistence, employ it to good purpose, but as a lash upon Mr. Flower.'[93]

At a local level, Cambridge itself exemplified most of the political evils and corruption that Flower condemned during his decade as editor. Prior to 1780 Cambridge was not a pocket borough. There had been a lively election contest in 1774; the mayor did not have unfettered power and Dissenters were allowed to become Corporation members. All this changed as a result of the ambitions of two young men, John Mortlock and the Duke of Rutland, who campaigned in the reform movement of the 1770s, became firm friends and political accomplices and ended by getting control of the borough in the 1780s.[94] Meanwhile Rutland's rival, the Earl of Hardwicke, dominated the county. It was primarily against the Hardwicke interest that Flower concentrated his attacks.[95] Under Mortlock, mayor of the town thirteen times before his death in 1816, there was a marked deterioration in the conduct of the Corporation, with corruption and inefficiency increasing. Candidates nominated by Rutland and backed by Mortlock were returned unopposed for the borough until 1818. Mortlock founded the famous Rutland Club at 'The Eagle' public house in Bene't Street, opposite his own house and bank, so that he might entertain the magistrates, councillors and Corporation members who supported the Rutland interest in the town. Under the circumstances borough elections, according to Flower, were little more than 'a farce', the whole election procedure merely amounting to 'a few men appointed in an arbitrary manner by an individual well paid by the Government, choosing two representatives for a populous town, in which a large majority of the inhabitants are not suffered to vote.' What were termed elections were 'succeeded as usual by feasting and carousing and plenty of beer was distributed out of doors.'[96]

The highlight of these war years in Cambridge however was the 1802 election when Lord C.S. Manners attempted to regain some of the family's former power in the county.[97] The independent candidate, Sir Henry Peyton, quickly withdrew, according to Flower, to ensure that the hard-pressed representative of the Hardwicke interest, Charles Yorke, got the nomination.[98] Hoping to see the overthrow of the Yorkes, Flower was outraged by the manoeuvres that induced Peyton to retire and he condemned the 'ministerial high Church junta' that supported and campaigned for Yorke.[99] After the election of both Yorke and Rutland for the county, Flower published an *Address to the Freeholders* in which he launched a blistering attack on Yorke's reputation and politics.[100] He was condemned for his unquestioning support of Pitt and the war, for accepting increasing taxation and attacks on printers, for a short-sighted and repressive Irish policy and above all for the corruption practised at the recent election.[101] The truth was that the Yorkes were losing their hold on the county representation, partly because of ill-feeling caused by their involvement in the expensive Eau Brink scheme to improve the navigation between Cambridge and King's Lynn and the subsequent raising of rents. The result was that Yorke was forced to withdraw from the 1810 election primarily because of his growing unpopularity among the county freeholders,[102] and Lord Francis Godolphin Osborne, the nominee of the Duke of Bedford, was elected. Flower and the Cambridge-based opposition had given the family a most difficult time during the recent election. It had proved both expensive and embarrassing;[103] Yorke admitted in a letter to his half-brother 'I think I have never been so harassed in my life.' His rescue by the retirement of Peyton, 'so bitterly complained of by the leading Dissenters',[104] proved a short reprieve, and his final address of thanks printed in the Tory *Chronicle* is an epitaph on the decline of the Hardwickes from a position of consequence in the state in the eighteenth century to one of impotence in their county by the early nineteenth.[105]

Reform was not the only political issue during these years. Religion also proved a vitally interesting topic, especially in the University. The most celebrated case to appear in the Cambridge press in the early years was undoubtedly that of William Frend, Fellow of Jesus College, who became a convert to Unitarianism[106] —a change of religion which was neither understood nor appreciated in the stronghold of the established Church. Flower arrived too late on the scene to be of any help to Frend in his struggle against University authority,[107] but he continued the tradition of opposition to the established Church and especially to Charles Simeon, William Wilberforce and the new Evangelical party which was gradually gaining acceptance as a powerful minority group within the University.[108] Disappointed at their failure to get a repeal of the Test and Corporation Acts in 1789 and 1790 and embittered by the opposition of Pitt, Burke and Wilberforce, Flower and other Dissenters hardened their hearts against the Church and State that had rejected them.[109] Their opposition, however, did not arise exclusively because of their legal disabilities. Dissent always had a close affinity in its philosophy with revolution – a fact their enemies would not let them forget.[110]

Flower was an Arian of the school of Price in theological matters.[111] He rejected all dogma and stressed conduct as the true touchstone of present liberty and eventual salvation. Unitarians accepted the Biblical narrative but denied both the divinity and deity of Christ, and this subverted the whole Christian scheme of salvation. Though Arians accepted a slightly less radical view this transferred the vital emphasis from faith to works, from salvation by divine grace to salvation by worthy conduct.[112] Flower therefore attacked bishops because they were unscriptural, and Wilberforce and his followers because of their support of the established Church, as well as their general opposition to religious liberation and freedom. As in most other cases the war was the true test of action and conduct for Flower, and here the Evangelicals stood condemned, perpetrating the idea of National Fasts[113] and 'showing their approbation of the present war of carnage and desolation.'[114] Their approval of the war went further than mere acceptance for 'there is scarcely a parish meeting advertised for the support of the war but we find a clergyman in the chair' especially 'those evangelical gentlemen.' These 'falsely termed evangelical brethren' could only be compared to the 'Pharisees of old' and especially their leader Wilberforce, 'high professor and eloquent writer on vital Christianity ... defender of a war which he firmly believes has sent millions of his fellow creatures into a state of eternal torment!!!'[115] Other denominations were little better; in France Roman Catholicism was no more than 'a shroud for atheism, infidelity and vice of every kind'; Presbyterians were 'no different to other establishments', and Methodists, with their arbitrary type of Church government, were 'more deeply criminal than the rest.'[116] The Quakers were the only exception Flower could find, and he praised them for their industry, humanity and opposition to the war.[117] They were also the only group that had always opposed the slave trade, and here Flower was prepared to give even the Evangelicals his support, his major criticism being that they did not pursue the matter whole-heartedly enough.

The abolition of the slave trade was a cause the Rational Dissenters always supported, believing as they did that it was part of the nature of the individual that he was free. Abolition in this sense was a religious crusade, and Robinson's Cambridge Constitutional Society was one of the first groups to petition Parliament against the trade. Those who participated in the movement, both leaders and followers, felt a religious compulsion to do so. By the time Flower began to print the *Intelligencer,* events in France had suffocated anti-slavery sentiment along with other liberal reform movements. Abolitionists were accused of being Jacobins, and most supporters were silenced during the decade that followed.[118] Not so Flower. He opposed the trade from the first issue of the *Intelligencer* to the last issue of his later publication, the *Political Review and Monthly Register,* in 1810.[119] The government, ministers and Parliament were condemned for not solving the problem: 'Thus is the public trifled with and Heaven insulted by our perseverence in a trade which no one ought to vindicate but a devil incarnate! If anything can add to our national guilt it must be our fasting and praying while we continue in this cause of villainy.'[120] The whole editorial of 7 March 1795 was devoted to the question: 'The Commons again having rejected a motion for abolition; the members returned as they went with their hands full of blood . . .' This state of affairs, he maintained, suited the Liverpool slave traders, but the ignoble trade, like the war, seemed destined to continue, occasionally discussed but never abolished, usually postponed so that the 'sincere' Mr. Pitt and the 'consistent' Mr. Wilberforce could quietly continue 'forging additional fetters for their countrymen at home.'[121]

There was, however, some equivocation in Flower's own early attitude to the slavery issue. Though he opposed the trade, he believed that 'an immediate and total emancipation of the negroes in the West Indies, would in the present uninformed state of that oppressed race of men, prove to them a curse, instead of a blessing.'[122] By 1799, however, he was condemning slavery in America, 'that boasted land of liberty', and urging the formation of an Association, with Wilberforce, Fox and the Thorntons at its head, in an effort to undermine the economy of the West Indies by persuading the public to refrain from purchasing West Indian produce.[123] Frustrated in his hopes of emancipation by parliamentary means, he was by 1801 advocating rebellion by the slaves as the only solution: 'we most sincerely hope that the Almighty Avenger will enable the oppressed to break their chains over the heads of their oppressors.'[124] The same sentiments are expressed when he heard of the negro insurrections in the West Indies: 'All our hopes of the abolition, we confess, now centre in the negroes THEMSELVES![125]

One of the most noticeable features of Flower's paper was his sympathetic support for those demanding a more liberal attitude to Ireland and Catholic emancipation. A surprising number of prominent Dissenters were anti-Catholic and in the 1780s Priestley, and now Flower, chided them for their inconsistency in claiming for themselves what they would deny to others.[126] However, Unitarians were more receptive to liberal ideas than most,[127] and in this matter, as in so many others, Flower was completely opposed to the University and town, and probably to the majority of the population of England at the time. He had no love for the Roman Catholic religion as such, but he vigorously defended the right of Catholics to have freedom to practise their religion and not be dominated, as they were in Ireland, by an alien established Church.[128] Politically, he felt the Irish were oppressed, deprived of their rights and deserving of a much more understanding approach from the English government. The Catholic question also involved a whole range of important problems in which Flower the radical was passionately interested — the nature of civil rights, the place of religion in the constitution of the state, the royal prerogative and the reform of government in Ireland. Unfortunately for Ireland, politicians found there was room for debate on all these problems and usually deadlock was the result. Flower realised that unless some bold and just solution was offered for the Anglo-Irish problem there might be dangerous consequences, mainly because it seemed the government was 'determined to drive that numerous and respectable body of men [the Irish Catholics] to a state of desperation.'[129] Flower set out to publicise Ireland's wrongs by printing extracts and comments from Irish newspapers and journals and occasionally even long speeches by Grattan on Anglo-Irish affairs.[130] He felt that no apology was necessary for reporting Irish affairs at such length, assured his readers that 'no exaggeration [was] made use of' and emphasised that, 'wretched as the conduct of our rulers has been in this kingdom, we find it, if possible, still worse in our sister kingdom', with the Irish suffering under what could only be justly described as 'a military despotism.'[131] Considering the situation,

> we wonder not at any desperate measures which the oppressed may resort to. Do the governors of any country wish to force the people to what is called Rebellion, (but which the history of this country proves that Britons have thought at times — LAWFUL RESISTANCE), they have only to establish a system of picketing, or torture; to banish men, or bury them in dungeons, without a trial; to seize their property, ruin their families, and burn their houses! We only wonder at the stupidity of rulers, when they expect obedience from a people thus treated.[132]

When the inevitable rebellion occurred in 1798, Flower condemned the way it was suppressed and pleaded for leniency on behalf of the Irish because of the brutality of the system that had driven them to such desperate measures.[133] He was now more convinced than ever that a radical reform of the corrupt Irish constitution was the only solution. When Pitt proposed a union of the two nations, Flower stressed that 'No Union or conciliatory proposals will ever be effectual, unless Catholic Emancipation, and relief, from the crying and scandalous oppression of Tythes, form the foundation.'[134] From Ireland's point of view there appeared little attraction in a political union and as she was already economically and religiously unfree he could not understand why Pitt was demanding the final concession. He reminded the Irish that, whatever the inducement offered, it could not 'recompense a free country for the loss of its independence.'[135] Pitt's determination ensured the passage of the act but the King's conscience denied the Irish their promised emancipation. Flower could only express stunned disappointment at the whole unhappy sequence of events.[136] His outspoken opposition to government policy in Ireland, and his championing of the cause of the Irish, is the more noteworthy when one realises that he was in custody and imprisoned for libel from May to October 1799.[137]

Flower's case arose out of an earlier attack by the Unitarian divine Gilbert Wakefield [138] on a publication by Richard Watson, Bishop of Llandaff, one of the first of the democratic circle to apostatize.[139] Watson had been prominent in the reform movement in Cambridge in the 1780s[140] but now he was an absentee; he was also a pluralist, his duties as Regius Professor of Divinity at Cambridge were performed by Dr. Kipling who had helped prosecute William Frend. Wakefield's reply to this publication led not only to his own imprisonment but also to that of his publisher and bookseller. Flower was arrested in April 1799 for defending Wakefield. He was fined one hundred pounds and sentenced to six months' imprisonment in Newgate, for contempt, by the House of Lords, for describing Llandaff in an editorial as 'the Right Reverend time server and apostate.'[141] The Unitarian author George Dyer, a former tutor in the family of Robert Robinson, was later imprisoned for coming to Flower's defence. A subscription was raised to discharge Flower's expenses, which amounted to four hundred pounds, and it is a comment on the circulation of his newspaper, and a recognition of his radical stand that from the town of Liverpool (which was a stronghold of Unitarianism) 'where the editor knew not an individual', ninety pounds was collected. Cambridge contributed a mere twenty-five pounds.[142] The whole episode looks suspiciously like a very efficient mopping up operation of the most important of the Dissenters.[143] As a result many more began to disengage themselves from political activism. Two years later Wakefield emerged from prison weakened in health to die almost at once of fever. Flower himself had second thoughts about continuing the newspaper because of the renewed possibility of 'loss of Liberty and the ruin of his circumstances for the faint and distant prospect of doing good to his countrymen.'[144] Another factor which may have prompted this consideration was his marriage, shortly after his release, to Miss Eliza Gould, an independent and self-reliant disciple of his who had also suffered for her liberal opinions.[145]

Nevertheless, once released from Newgate, he continued as before, attacking the war and the government, the slave trade and established religion. But by now it was becoming clear that Flower was suffering the agony of disillusionment. He was usually willing to support Fox the reformer: 'Until, however, the people at large second Mr. Fox's efforts, we cannot but think that great man perfectly justifiable in not wasting his time, and talents in unavailing efforts to save a people, equally insensible and ungrateful.'[146] Monumental indifference was widespread, and 'corruption and absence of principle seems to have affected almost all sects and parties. Not only ministers of the established Church, but those who dissent from it, have flagrantly apostasized from their principles, and are floating down the general tide, unable to vindicate their conduct though persevering in their criminal course. Character and consistency of conduct, now appear to be little expected, and less regarded . . .'[147] He saw little possibility of an honourable peace, but when peace came in October 1801 it was 'the more grateful as it is unexpected.' However, after years of war and bloodshed, nothing had been gained . . . 'We feel for the humiliation of our country, but at the same time we cannot but REJOICE, that by the return of PEACE, we have some hope left of rescue from utter ruin.'[148] His hopes were shortlived. With the impending threat of a return to war in 1803 he decided the time had come to retire from the political fray, depressed as he was by the 'Mighty Ruin which threatens Our Dear, Our Guilty, Our Unfortunate Country!'[149] He left Cambridge in 1804 and established himself in business at Harlow in Essex, where he printed some of the works of his favourite Divine, Robert Robinson.[150]

The attraction of politics, however, proved irresistible, and in 1807, 'at the desire of several readers of a late provincial print, *The Cambridge Intelligencer*', he launched a new journal entitled *Flower's Political Review and Monthly Register.*[151] This was a more ambitious undertaking, offering not only an elaboration of Flower's political and religious views but also a more detailed political commentary on current affairs, State Papers and parliamentary proceedings, while also including 'a Review of the principal publications relating to general Politics, and Civil and Religious liberty.'[152] Thomas Hardy stated that it was popular among London radicals and held 'very deservedly in high estimation'. He urged Flower to continue publication and encouraged friends to subscribe to the *Review*.[153] Flower's opening editorial stressed the two most powerful forces in his life – Religion and Government – 'the two chief concerns of a rational creature; the one embracing his interest in time, and the other his interests for eternity . . . Although divine revelation was never designed to instruct us in the science of civil government, or in the nature of the different modes by which it may be administered, it clearly lays down and powerfully enforces those principles and virtues, which if understood and practised, would lead men to peace, to freedom and to happiness.'[154] The permanent quotation printed under the title of the *Register* reinforced these sentiments: 'What is morally wrong can never be politically right.'[155]

While continuing his attacks on the government, the parties,[156] the slave trade and the war,[157] he was as firm as ever in his advocacy of religious toleration and freedom of conscience. Though William Cobbett enjoyed much general popularity, he stood condemned in Flower's eyes for his 'detestible principles respecting the slave trade, and the education of the poor . . . his despotic maritime code' as well as his patriotic attitude to the war with France.[158] On the other hand: 'It is to the honour of Napoleon, that he has uniformly proved the friend of religious toleration.'[159] Though disappointed at the response of other Protestant Dissenters, he continued his support for Catholic emancipation: 'Reason and religion therefore, equally demand . . . the catholics of Ireland, ought no longer to remain in a state of proscription, but to be restored to the full enjoyment of their civil rights. All the reasons which induced our ancestors to regard the catholics with a jealous eye are vanished . . .'[160] Justice for Ireland was important but the absolute necessity of negotiations for peace remained paramount for there was reason to hope 'that by PEACE, followed by a system of ECONOMY and REFORM, we might in some measure retrieve our misfortunes, and, amidst the wreck of the continental states, preserve our own independence.'[161] Flower was now increasingly reluctant to continue his apparently futile literary and political efforts, and after the death of his wife in childbirth in 1810 he published the final volume in July of that year.[162] Soon after, he retired to his family home in Dalston, where he died in 1829 leaving two highly gifted daughters, Eliza and Sarah.[163]

Despite eventual disillusionment Flower could look back with pride on his journalistic contribution.[164] There can be no doubt that he proved an inspiration during this period for many reformers and encouraged in Cambridge the founding of another radical newspaper in 1819 which continued to preach the political and religious ideals he had advocated in more difficult circumstances.[165] Though deeply influenced by the French Revolution, Flower reached back into the dissenting and libertarian traditions of the eighteenth century for his inspiration, finding it in the completely English Rational dissenting tradition of men such as Price and Robinson, while occasionally sharpening it with a touch of Painite radicalism, thereby distinguishing it from such Whiggish Radicalism as, for example, that of Edward Baines of *The Leeds Mercury*.[166] He was one of the few who ensured that popular radicalism was not entirely extinguished when the

Corresponding societies were broken up and all 'Jacobin' manifestations outlawed.[167] He then kept the radical flame alight for ten years despite the opposition of both University and Town, six months imprisonment and the exceptional problems involved in running a provincial newspaper with a national circulation. During this decade his journalistic contribution was unique. E.P. Thompson rightly refers to *The Cambridge Intelligencer* as 'the last national organ of intellectual Jacobinism.'[168] Flower was the only provincial editor consistently to denounce the French War and advocate peace, civil and religious liberty and reform, with his own brand of candour and conviction. Furthermore, his development of the editorial as a method of disseminating radical political and religious views gives him an important place in the history of provincial journalism at a time when it was obviously wiser to reflect, rather than to try to shape, political opinion in English society.

III

Politics and religion were important issues during the late eighteenth century but the newspapers also provide a vivid record of social and economic change during this vital period of transition in English history and there is plenty of evidence to suggest that the improving spirit of the period was not just the preserve of the industrial Midlands and North. These 'improvements' tended to fascinate and alarm contemporaries and though the word now sounds rather sober and respectable it was a highly emotive one at the time, stimulating great flights of imagination and general optimism for the future. Though Cambridge was a university town, with no coal fields within fifty miles, its newspapers contain an abundance of examples illustrating contemporary social problems especially with regard to population growth and its attendant problems of public health, housing and poverty, agricultural change and so on. Social change is accepted as having occurred most rapidly in the industrial areas of England, but Cambridge shared, at least to some extent, the challenges and problems posed by the growth and development of the new industrial society. There was also plenty of scope for economic gain through agricultural improvement in the county, particularly as a rising national population meant an increase in demand for both wheat and meat, while improved transport facilities could help reduce costs and widen markets. The controversy surrounding the Eau Brink Cut is a good example of the interest which could be aroused, and the clash of interests that could be precipitated in town and county, by such an improvement. This issue was discussed and debated at length in the Cambridge press during this period. At a time when letters to the press were rare, there were sometimes as many as five letters concerning the proposed Cut in a weekly edition.[169]

Geography had made Cambridge an important place on the map, and the river Cam, winding through the Fenland to join the Ouse, gave the town its wealth. The town's 'port' was King's Lynn and therefore the state of the navigation from Cambridge to the Wash always attracted notice. As early as 1781 it was noted that navigation by barges was in danger of being severely obstructed by the silting of the channel between Cambridge and Clayhithe, and an Act for its improvement was passed in 1783.[170] This defect illustrated another of the major difficulties of the southern Fenland — the continued lack of drainage facilities. Not only the fen rivers, such as the Cam and Ouse, but their outfalls became more and more choked with tidal silts. Water mills were extensively used to try to relieve the problem, but were never really adequate for the task. The outfall towns, such as King's Lynn, were always apprehensive about the state of their harbours, the dangers of sandbanks and silting, while the local landowners and gentry were more concerned about the position and efficiency of sluices on the rivers which drained their immediate area.

The best-known improver of the Fens was the Dutch engineer, Vermuyden, under whose direction cuts, drains and sluices were made in the seventeenth century. In 1642 he divided the fen area into three divisions — the North, Middle and South Levels. From 1697 each was a separate entity, responsible for its own government, raising the necessary revenue for improvement and controlling and supervising the work of drainage. With the consequent multiplicity of local unco-ordinated efforts, on short stretches of river or areas of fen supervision, maintenance was extremely haphazard. Darby states, 'there was everywhere a chaos of authorities and an absence of authority.'[171] Divided and often clashing interests, the failure to agree on comprehensive programmes of drainage and navigation improvement, accounted for the very slow progress of drainage, and the bad conditions prevailing throughout most of the three Levels.

In the South Level, Cambridge was primarily worried about the navigation of the Ouse down to King's Lynn, and in the late eighteenth century therefore, tended to favour schemes such as the Eau Brink Cut for improving this stretch of river. The merchants of King's Lynn, however, while in general welcoming improvement schemes, were equally anxious that any improvement of this tidal river should not prove detrimental to the harbour. The farmers of the three Levels were uncertain whether their lands would be helped or harmed by the Cut or how the rates should be apportioned between the various regions. It was clear to everybody that the Ouse itself was getting wider and shallower, and that sluices, such as the Denver Sluice, were not efficient at regulating it. In 1751 Nathaniel Kinderley suggested that the real problems of the river were caused by the large bend in the Ouse three miles outside the port of King's Lynn.[172] This rambling, circuitous course, expanding to a width of nearly a mile, often through sandbanks and broken shallows, was obviously a hazard to navigation. The Rev. William Gooch commented on the consequent evils. Internal navigation was rendered so defective 'that boats cannot pass from German's Bridge to Lynn without pilots', which caused both delays and extra freight charges. The banks of the river had to be repaired and maintained at 'an enormous expense' and drainage was so impeded that 'many thousands of acres are now under water.' Furthermore, because of the resultant beds of sand, only boats of a certain draught could operate between the port of Lynn and the sea, and consequently 'foreign trade is enjoyed by a small number of merchants who are their own carriers, and the price of coals, raft etc. is considerably higher in Lynn than it ought to be.'[173] It was suggested that a direct channel from Eau Brink to King's Lynn harbour would eliminate the six-mile detour, improving both the

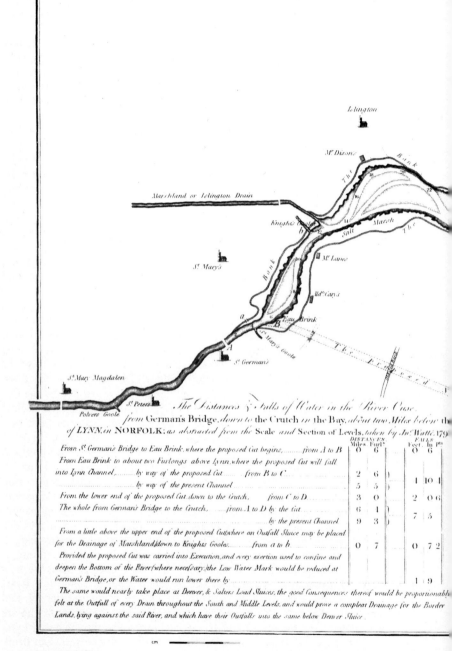

The Distances & Falls of Water in the River Ouse, from German's Bridge, down to the Crutch in the Bay, about two Miles below the town of LYNN, in NORFOLK; as abstracted from the Scale and Section of Levels, taken by Jn.º Watté. 179_

	DISTANCES Miles Furl.ˢ		FALLS Feet. In. P.ᵗˢ		
From S.ᵗ German's Bridge to Eau Brink, where the proposed Cut begins, ... from A to B	0	6	0	6	
From Eau Brink to about two Furlongs above Lynn, where the proposed Cut will fall into Lynn Channel, ... by way of the proposed Cut .... from B to C	2	6	1	10	4
.... by way of the present Channel	5	5			
From the lower end of the proposed Cut down to the Crutch, ... from C to D	3	0	2	0	6
The whole from German's Bridge to the Crutch, ... from A to D by the Cut	6	1	7	5	
.... by the present Channel	9	3			
From a little above the upper end of the proposed Cut where an Outfall Sluice may be placed for the Drainage of Marshland, down to Knights Goolas .... from a to h	0	7	0	7	2
Provided the proposed Cut was carried into Execution, and every exertion used to confine and deepen the Bottom of the River where necessary; the Low Water Mark would be reduced at German's Bridge, or the Water would run lower there by			1	9	

The same would nearly take place at Denver, & Salters Load Sluices, the good Consequences thereof would be proportionably felt at the Outfall of every Drain throughout the South and Middle Levels, and would prove a compleat Drainage for the Border Lands, lying against the said River, and which have their Outfalls into the same below Denver Sluice.

Eau Brink Cut

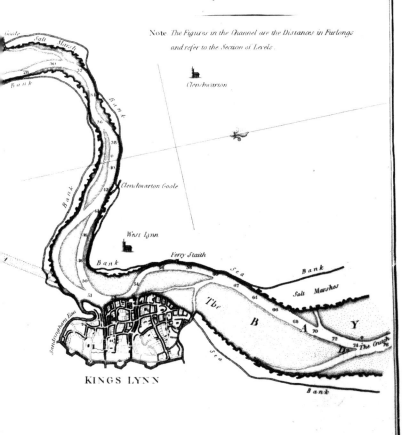

A Sketch or —

MAP of LYNN HAVEN,

and of the

River Oufe to S.! Mary Magdalen,

shewing the

Propofed New Cut.

Note *The Figures in the Channel are the Distances in Furlongs and refer to the Section of Levels.*

Tilney

Goole Salt Marsh

Bank

28

30

32

Clenchwarton

34

Bank

36

38

40

Bank

42 Clenchwarton Goole

44

Bank

46 West Lynn

48 Ferry Stauth

Bank 56 58 Sea Bank

50 54 60 62 Salt Marshes

51 64

The 66 Sea

Sandringham Eau 68 B A Y

KINGS LYNN 70

72

74 The Crutch

76

Sea

Bank

gradient and the scour of the river. Internal navigation would be safer and cheaper, drainage easier and foreign trade open to all. 'In a word,' a correspondent to the *Chronicle* stated, 'Navigation, Drainage and Agriculture will be amazingly benefited, and Trade and Commerce so altered that coals, raft and other goods will be infinitely cheaper, to the great benefit of the consumer.'[174]

The opposition to the proposed scheme claimed that none of these benefits would result. Thomas Hyde Page, one of the many engineers who surveyed the river, contended that Lynn would suffer because the 'wide circuitous course gave room for tides', which if confined in a straight cut would fill the port with silt and sand. There was also doubt whether the banks of the Cut would be able to hold 'a current so fast and capricious.'[175] Conflicting reports from engineers such as Watté, Milne and Golborne, simply added to the confusion.[176]

The merchants of Lynn were opposed to the Cut, as were certain landowners, particularly in the South Level, who maintained they would have to pay taxes to finance the Cut and yet receive little or no benefit.[177] They claimed in a letter to the Earl of Hardwicke[178] that their lands comprised nearly half the number of acres to be taxed, yet there was no guarantee that the new Cut would improve drainage to any considerable extent in the South Level. Primarily because of remarks made by anonymous writers to the *Cambridge Chronicle* he, in turn, was forced to write a tract explaining his support for the scheme. Despite the opposition of various landowners and merchants, he believed it 'an object of great importance, in a national view, to bring into a state of more certain cultivation, a considerable tract of country, the product of which is comparatively small.' He defended the engineers whom he felt had been 'badly treated in an effort to discredit their reports' and donated £500 to help lesser landowners pay the proposed taxes. However, on the main issue he remained adamant, insisting that 'unless something is done all the estates will in the course of a few years be of little value.'[179] A writer to the *Chronicle* noted with similar concern 'that the violent contention between the two parties seems likely to cripple, if it does not totally destroy, a noble project.'[180]

Four years after Golborne's optimistic report of 1791, and despite some vociferous fen opposition, an Act of Parliament was passed empowering the Bedford Level to levy rates on land, and tolls on shipping, to finance the Cut; and set up separate but overlapping Commissioners of Drainage and of Navigation to build and administer it. Only after the French Wars, however, did work get under way. In 1817 John Rennie was appointed chief engineer or, more accurately, one of the chief engineers. He represented the drainage faction and Thomas Telford represented the navigation interests. The engineers who worked on the Cut were among the leaders of their profession, the makers of great canals and of four London bridges. Work began in 1818 and was soon, according to the *Chronicle*, 'proceeding with a rapidity unprecedented in the annals of Drainage', and 'a thousand men and hundreds of carts and horses' were being employed. A fine new bridge was also built over the Cut at King's Lynn. A steam pumping engine weighing twenty two tons was used on the scheme, (constructed by Boulton & Watt at a cost of £1200), one of the earliest applications of steam power to fenland drainage.[181] The Cut was eventually completed at a

cost of almost £500,000 in 1821, and although it had an immediate and beneficial effect, it was not as great an improvement as had been expected.[182] The
first report presented to the Commissioners by the engineers pointed out that 'on
account of the inadequate dimensions of the New Cut the banks on both sides
are considerably injured . . . that the shoals near the town[Lynn] are upon the
increase' and unless these defects were remedied the situation would worsen.[183]
The news provoked much controversy and reopened the whole question once
more in the newspapers.

The Ouse Navigation Commissioners, backed by the merchants of Lynn and
the farmers of the Middle Level, therefore decided to submit a new bill demanding that all these defects be remedied. This bill was opposed by almost every
other interested party in the South Level, mainly because of the extra cost
involved. The *Cambridge Independent Press* under Weston Hatfield, which
devoted much of its energy to reporting fen affairs, supported the farming
interests of the South Level and stated that the new bill was almost 'irrecon-
cilable with justice' as the proposed measure had 'no limit to taxation while
the advantages it holds out to the county are but equivocal.'[184] A meeting of the
fen proprietors was called at Ely and 'the powerful interest excited through the
Fens' was demonstrated by the hundreds of horsemen and carriages that 'covered
the roads leading to the city', as over a thousand proprietors made their way to
the meeting.[185] Their opposition defeated the bill in 1825. As a result the Eau
Brink Drainage Commissioners agreed to 'the immediate widening of the new
Cut and the closing of the lower dam' on an understanding that the opposition
would refrain from 'Parliamentary or legal proceedings, til three years experience
has been had of the effect of these measures.'[186] When work commenced two
years later, the *Chronicle* hailed the new conciliatory measure between the
drainage and navigation interests as 'one of the greatest public improvements
to be effected in this part of the country for many years.' In 1830 it considered
the whole scheme a success because 'floods have passed away without doing any
material damage to the Fens . . . The improvement of the outfall, through the
Eau Brink works, has been strikingly shown.'[187]

It might appear that East Anglia, with its flat terrain would prove a major
centre of canal building, but this was not the case. The Fens were already
intersected in all directions by cuts, for the dual purpose of drainage and navigation and as a result only one minor canal was built during the period — from
Wisbech to Outwell. In 1781 the Navigation Committee of London proposed the
building of a canal linking the river Thames with the Cam via Bishop's Stortford.[188] The hope was expressed that Cambridge might become 'the Eastern
Centre of a most extensive inland commerce', but the bill was not introduced
into Parliament until 1810. An immense increase in trade was confidently
predicted in 'stone, lime, coals, various minerals, timber, malt, wheat, and various
grains, manures and numerous species of merchandize.'[189] The cost was estimated
at £200,000 and the plan was enthusiastically received by the Earl of Hardwicke
and other county agricultural progressives, such as the Rev. Leworthy of Harston,
the most vociferous defender of the scheme in the local press.[190] It was opposed
by the Cambridge Corporation because it feared the canal would interfere with

the water supply to Hobson's Conduit; by some landed gentry who were nervous that water would be drained from their lands; by local road carriers such as James Burleigh, and by the barge masters, brewers and traders of Bishop's Stortford who feared their depot facilities would be bypassed and rendered unnecessary.[191] Public meetings at Royston and Fulbourn voted in favour of constructing the canal but the bill was defeated in Committee in 1811.[192] Undaunted, the canal proposers made certain concessions, re-routing the canal through Saffron Walden. However, as estimated costs doubled and technical difficulties mounted, interest and support gradually dwindled. Though the second bill was passed by Parliament in 1812, the canal was never constructed. A correspondent to the *Chronicle* put the case for Town and Gown when he stated that 'the characteristic of Cambridge is the seat of Learning not Trade. And who has not lamented the heterogeneous mixture of barges with gownsmen in her college walks, troubling her waters and disturbing her quiet in the language of Billingsgate; and heaping upon her banks the whole produce of the Fens to be dispersed through the county? To supply her wants may she shall have her Cam! But let the channel for foreign traffic be turned aside to a more respectful distance.'[193]

The improvements in draining that characterised the period were paralleled to some extent by improvements in agricultural techniques. There was plenty of scope for these in a county where two thirds of the land remained either open field or waste and unimproved fen. There is evidence for some claying of lighter soils, deep ploughing, the introduction of water mills and increased use of the threshing machine.[194] Despite the example set by Lord Hardwicke in these matters and the founding of the Cambridge Agricultural Society in 1811, progress was extremely slow, primarily because fen farmers appeared more reluctant than most to abandon traditional methods. This situation earned the county a poor reputation among national improvers. Both Vancouver in 1794 and Gooch in 1813 deplored the general state of agriculture in a county where the open field system was still in existence as late as 1900.[195] Some however, were convinced of the benefits of enclosure and under the stimulus of high prices during the Napoleonic Wars a start was made. Over seventy Acts of Parliament enclosing land in the county (the majority dealing with areas of about 1500 to 2000 acres) were passed between 1796 and 1815.[196] In key enclosure years, such as 1801 and 1811, enclosure notices gave a welcome boost to newspaper revenue, often covering the whole of the front page of the *Chronicle*.[197] Most letters to the press condemned enclosures, often blaming them for much of the discontent, scarcity, rioting and distress which characterised the war years, and lament the destruction of 'the chain which held rural society together.'[198] Hodson argued that enclosures were improvements that would alleviate poverty and dismissed as erroneous statements that claimed that the loss of common land harmed the poor. His opinion was 'the more extensive the commons in a district, the more miserable the poor.'[199]

The town of Cambridge also had to contend with enclosures, and here, as in the county, these improvements were received with a mixture of approval and opposition. Commoners' rights were extinguished in 1801 when the endowers of

Downing College enclosed the lands called St. Thomas Leys. The following year it was the turn of Cambridge Field to the north-west of the town. The most important of the town enclosure acts, however, was the Barnwell Enclosure Act of 1807 which led to the most pronounced urban development over the next fifty years.[200] Most of the land involved belonged to the trustees of Thomas Panton and the remainder to Jesus College. The trustees quickly auctioned their holdings to local builders who proceeded to erect terraced housing for the working-class of the town in the Newmarket Road and Fitzroy Street areas. The horticultural area known as the 'Garden of Eden' was developed in the 1820s and 1830s and the new streets appropriately named Adam & Eve Street, Eden Street and Paradise Street. The other major area of working-class housing was the New Town area between Hills Road and Trumpington Road — designated a slum within a decade of its creation. Some middle-class housing was also built north of the river in Chesterton and near the Huntingdon Road but by the 1840s speculative interest was already moving towards Mill Road and the Romsey Town area which was near the railway.

An unusual feature of the development of housing in Cambridge was the continued mixing of working and middle-class houses in the newly developed area, for example Brookside and New Town, Maid's Causeway and Barnwell. Most of the working-class housing rapidly deteriorated into slum accommodation. Demand constantly outran supply (the population of Barnwell grew from 252 in 1800 to 9,486 in 1841)[201] and conditions in the worst areas of the town differed little from those in industrial areas. In the absence, therefore, of either civic or philanthropic effort directed to the improvement of social conditions, the new town began to grow up in a haphazard fashion and little care was taken to render it habitable. New cottages were crammed into available quarters of the old town, and as the network of small streets spread further and further health problems were left to solve themselves. As late as 1849 it was calculated that one sixth of the population was living in small courts, alleys and yards, many under conditions of extreme overcrowding, without drainage, ventilation or water supply. Typhoid, scarlet fever, smallpox and cholera were the natural concomitants of such conditions. In 1849 one of the newly appointed health inspectors observed that 'the sanitary condition of numerous courts and places is so wretched as to be a disgrace to humanity, and still more so to civilisation.'[202]

A complementary development was a rapid increase in the number of poor in the town. Treatment of the poor was still based on the Elizabethan Act of 1601 and with some alterations this act formed the basis of Poor Law administration until 1834. Briefly, it established the parish as the basic unit of organisation, appointed local overseers, ordered the levying of a compulsory poor-rate, statutory work for the unemployed and the building of Houses of Correction for the deliberately idle.[203] Cambridge, with fourteen parishes, found it difficult to organise its Poor Law system and having failed to build a general town workhouse in 1785 the Corporation simply allowed the parish almshouses to continue to manage as best they could. In fact, it was the poorhouse rather than the workhouse that was typical of Cambridge and in some parishes no workhouses existed.[204] Both newspapers were critical of the existing system as few workhouses made any pretence of organizing work and almost all of them were laxly supervised. In 1804 the workhouse population numbered a little over one hundred with nearly five times that number receiving outdoor relief.[205]

The problem was aggravated by the Napoleonic War and with the resultant scarcity, distress and the threat of riots the poor suddenly received the attention of the ruling interests in town and county. The *Chronicle* welcomed subscriptions for food and blankets and advocated Corporation subsidies to hold down the price of bread. In 1795 a hungry mob 'seized a lighter laden with flour which was going down the river to Ely' and only dispersed when the mayor agreed to use the flour for bread which he promised would be sold at a reduced price.[206] The following year Parliament agreed that the poor rate could be used to subsidise the wages of those whose incomes fell below subsistence level. The amount of this subsidy depended on the price of bread and certainly helped to alleviate some of the worst distress during the years that followed.[207] Nevertheless, as a correspondent stated in 1800, 'there are certain families in this town in inconceivable distress. Parish officers frequently know not what to do; the poor rates are already so high.'[208] No lasting solution to the problem emerged and soon magistrates at General Quarter Sessions voiced their concern at 'the enormous increase in the number of vagrants, who are constantly infesting the town and neighbourhood.'[209] The University Vice-Chancellor condemned 'the extraordinary influx of Beggars and Vagrants, who constantly infest the streets, walks and colleges, and give serious cause of alarm lest some outrage should be committed by them,'[210] A 'Society for the Suppression of Mendicity' was founded in 1819 but piecemeal humanitarian and administrative efforts proved a failure. Drastic rethinking was necessary and the developments of the 1790s stimulated a debate which reached its culmination in the Poor Law Report of 1834.

The town was fortunate in having an infirmary built in 1766. This was first endowed by John Addenbrooke and with the aid of subscriptions was soon converted into a general hospital to cater for the poor of the county. By 1827 beds were available for about fifty in-patients and in a busy week the hospital often treated as many as four hundred out-patients. The local press showed a keen interest in the common affairs of the hospital[211] but the issue which attracted most public attention was the proposed introduction of vaccination against smallpox.[212] The town physician Dr. Thackeray, who favoured its introduction, was opposed in the columns of the press by Sir Isaac Pennington, Professor of Physic at the University.[213] Many doctors wrote to the *Chronicle* urging the adoption of this improvement and opposed what they described as the reactionary approach of a man divorced from the realities of town life.[214] By 1818 they had won the day and vaccination appeared to be common practice.[215] Recent research has demonstrated how easy it is to exaggerate the imagined benefits resulting from these 'improvements' in the late eighteenth century. With such low standards of hygiene and medical expertise one was often more at risk in a hospital than outside![216] Improvements in environment such as replacement of timber by brick, clean water supply, better sewage disposal and drainage facilities would probably have had a more beneficial effect on town health than many of the 'improvements' so earnestly debated in the press during these years.

NOTES AND REFERENCES

1 See P.A. Brown, *The French Revolution in English History* (1918).
2 G.A. Williams, *Artisans and sans-culottes* (1968), Chs. 1, 4; E.C. Black, *The Association* (1963), pp. 223-31; E.P. Thompson, *The Making of the English Working Class* (1963), Chs. 4, 5.
3 F.K. Donnelly & J.L. Baxter, 'Sheffield and the English Revolutionary Tradition 1791-1820' in *International Review of Social History* (XX) 1975, pp. 398-423.
4 Williams, *Artisans*, p. 64.
5 Collet, *Taxes on Knowledge* I, p. 14; A. Andrews, *The History of British Journalism*, I, (1859), pp. 71-72.
6 Williams, *Artisans*, p. 76; Black, *Association*, p. 267.
7 *Camb. Chron.* 4 Jan. 1793.
8 A. Aspinall, *Politics and the Press* (1949), Ch. 3.
9 *Camb. Chron.* 22 Feb. 1793, 22 May 1802.
10 B. Flower, *Statement of the Facts* (1808), p. XXIII. See also *Dictionary of National Biography*, VII.
11 Thompson, *Making of the English Working Class*, pp. 451, 476; D. Read, *Press and People* (1961), pp. 69-70.
12 The following account of Flower's life is based on his own *Statement of the Facts*, an obituary notice in *The Monthly Repository*, New Series, III (1829), pp. 210-12, and *Dictionary of National Biography* VII, p. 339.
13 B. Flower, *The French Constitution* (1792).
14 Read, *Press and People*, pp. 69-70; F.J. Hinkhouse, *The Preliminaries of the American Revolution as seen in the English Press 1763-1775* (1926), p. 11.
15 Black, *Association*, pp. 63-64, 180; D.M. Clark, *British Opinion and the American Revolution* (1930), p. 4; R.R. Rea, *The English Press in Politics 1760-1774* (1973), p. 199; G. Rudé, *Wilkes and Liberty* (1962), pp. 122-34.
16 *New Monthly Magazine*, xlviii (1836), p. 137; See also H.R. Fox Bourne, *English Newspapers* I, p. 379.
17 C. Mitchell, *Newspaper Press Directory* (1846), p. 123; Andrews, *History of British Journalism*, II, pp. 123, 286; J. Grant, *The Newspaper Press*, III, (1871-2), pp. 376-77; Read, *Press and People*, pp. 69-70.
18 H.W. Stephenson, *The Author of Nearer, my God, to Thee* (1922), pp. 2-9.
19 B. Nutter, *The Story of the Cambridge Baptists* (1912), Ch. IX.
20 Read, *Press and People*, Ch. III; R.V. Holt, *The Unitarian Contribution to Social Progress in England* (1938).

21 W.H.G. Armytage, 'The Editorial Experiences of Joseph Gales 1786-1794', in *North Carolina Historical Review* XXVIII, (1951).

22 B. Flower, *National Sins Considered in two letters to the Rev. T. Robinson* (1796), p. viii, D.M. Thompson, (ed.), *Nonconformity in the nineteenth century* (1972), pp. 6, 16, 17.

23 *Cambridge Intelligencer,* 24 June 1798 (hereafter abbreviated to *Camb. Int.*)

24 A. Lincoln, *Some Political and Social Ideas of English Dissent* (1938), p. 30.

25 For Unitarian periodicals see F.E. Mineka, *The Dissidence of Dissent: the Monthly Repository 1806-1838* (1944); H.McLachlan, *The Unitarian Movement in the Religious Life of England* (1934).

26 *Camb. Chron.* 11 Nov. 1774, 4, 11 Mar. 1780, 29 Jan., 11 June 1785.

27 *Ibid.* 16 Feb., 18 Mar. 1788; Lincoln, *English Dissent,* pp. 40-41; see also M.R. Adams, *Studies in the Literary Backgrounds of English Radicalism* (1947), pp. 233-34.

28 R.G. Cowherd, *The Politics of English Dissent* (1956), p. 64; U. Henriques, *Religious Toleration in England* (1961), pp. 25-32; R.N. Stromberg, *Religious liberalism in eighteenth-century England* (1954), pp. 37-39.

29 Lincoln, *English Dissent,* pp. 40-41, 44-45; Fox, *Monthly Repository,* p. 212.

30 See, for example, *Camb. Int.* 20 July, 31 Aug., 5 Oct., 1793, 13 Sept., 25 Oct., 1794, 24 Aug., 21, 28 Sept., 30 Nov. 1799; Stephenson, *Nearer, My God, To Thee,* pp. 7, 9.

31 *Camb. Int.* 14 June, 27 Sept., 11, 25 Oct., 1 Nov. 1794, 14 May, 17, 31 Dec. 1796, 6 Jan. 1798, 30 Oct. 1802.

32 Holt, *Unitarian Contribution,* pp. 116-17; *Camb. Int.* 25 Jan., 1794; H. McLachlan (ed.), *Letters of Theophilus Lindsey* (1920), pp.89-97, 126-30.

33 *Camb. Chron.* 25 Mar. 1780, 2 Oct. 1784; F. Knight, *University Rebel: the life of W. Frend* (1971), pp. 65-66.

34 *Camb. Int.* 18 June 1803; B. Flower, *The proceedings of the House of Lords in the case of Benjamin Flower* (1800), p. xxii.

35 *Camb. Int.* 6 Jan. 1798.

36 Merle, 'Provincial Press', p. 79.

37 *Camb. Int.* 27 Dec. 1794; 18 June 1803.

38 *Camb. Int.* 18 Jan. 1794, 18 June 1803. See also A. Temple Patterson, *Radical Leicester* (1954), pp. 16, 65, 110; W.R. Ward, *Religion and Society in England 1790-1850* (1972), Ch. 2.

39 *Camb. Int.* 26 Oct. 1799, 31 Jan., 20 June 1801.

40 E.S. Chalk, 'Circulation of XVIII – Century Newspapers' in *Notes and Queries,* vol. 169, (1935) p. 336.

41 W. Ashworth, *The Genesis of Modern British Town Planning* (1954), p. 31.

42 *Cambridge Independent Press,* 25 April 1829.

43 Fox, *Monthly Repository,* p. 210.

44 *Camb. Int.* 12 May 1798.

45 S.T. Coleridge, *The Watchman,* (ed. L. Patten), (1970), pp. 374-75.

46 Lincoln, *English Dissent,* pp. 37-38.

47 *Camb. Int.* 10 Aug. 1793.

48 *Ibid.* 19 July 1794.

49   *Ibid.* 2 Nov. 1793, 18 Jan. 1794, 18 April 1795, 7, 14 Feb. 1801.
50   *Ibid.* 18 Nov. 1797.
51   *Ibid.* 14 Mar. 1801.
52   *Ibid.* 17 Jan. 1794.
53   *Ibid.* 31 May 1794.
54   *Ibid.* 18 June 1803.
55   *Ibid.* 10 June 1797; Aspinall, *Politics and the Press,* pp. 22, 206, 449.
56   *Camb. Int.* 8, 22 Aug. 1801.
57   *Ibid.* 18 June 1803.
58   *Ibid.* 10 Aug. 1793.
59   *Ibid.* 22 Aug. 1801.
60   *Ibid.* 12 May 1798.
61   *Ibid.* 12 May 1798.
62   Knight, *University Rebel,* p. 190.
63   *Camb. Chron.* 22 Feb. 1793.
64   *Camb. Chron.* 24 Aug. 1793, 24 May, 1794.
65   *Ibid.* 27 Dec. 1794, 14 Jan. 1797, 22 May 1802.
66   *Cambridge Independent Press,* 25 April 1829; Cooper, *Annals* IV, pp. 445-46.
67   *Camb. Int.* 18 Jan. 1794.
68   Flower, *National Sins Considered,* p. IX.
69   Fox, *Monthly Repository,* p. 211.
70   *Camb. Int.* 23, 30 Jan, 1796, 6 Feb., 10 June 1797
71   *Ibid.* 28 Mar. 1795, 23 May, 16 Dec. 1797.
72   *Ibid.* 23 Nov. 1794, 19 Jan. 1799, 21 Nov. 1801.
73   *Camb. Int.* 19 April, 10, 17 May 1794; see also *Treasury Solicitors' Letters* 24.3.88 Public Record Office.
74   *Ibid.* 27 May 1797.
75   *Ibid.* 4 July 1795, 24 Aug. 1799.
76   C. Wyvill, *Political Papers* (1804), V, pp. 389-90, 399-400.
77   F.D. Cartwright, (ed.), *The Life and Correspondence of Major Cartwright,* I, (1826), p. 278.
78   *Camb. Int.* 27 May 1797.
79   J. Cannon, *Parliamentary Reform 1640-1832* (1973), p. 124.
80   *Camb. Int.* 16 Sept. 1797.
81   *Camb. Int.* 7 April, 1797, 26 Dec. 1801, 9 Jan., 20, 27 Mar. 1802.
82   Wyvill, *Political Papers,* V, pp. 70, 145-47, VI, pp. 7-9, 34-36, *Appendix* 1-57.
83   *Camb. Int.* 13 Sept. 1794. See also Mineka, *Dissidence of Dissent,* p. 23.
84   *Camb. Int.* 9 Aug. 1794.
85   *Ibid.* 15 Aug. 1795; 1 April, 27 May 1797.
86   P.R.O. *Letters and Papers* H.O. 42/26-71; *Domestic Entry Books* H.O. 43/4-13; *Law Officers' Reports* H.O. 119/1; *Secret Papers/Dissenters* H.O. 123/XIX. Also *Hardwicke Papers,* B.M., Add. MSS., 35392-35394, 35424 and *Hardwicke Papers,* Supplementary, 45040. For an analysis of problems involved in using Home Office material in the period 1790-1830, see Thompson, *Making of the English Working Class,* pp. 487-93.
87   H.O. 42/30, *Letter* 31 May 1794. Also 29 May 1794; H.O. 42/31, *Letters* 9, 14, 25 June 1794.
88   H.O. 42/29, *Letter* 29 April 1794.

89 H.O. 42/51, *Letter* 17 Sept. 1800.
90 *Ibid. Letter* 17 Sept. 1800.
91 H.O. 42/35, 27 July 1795.
92 *Hardwicke Papers,* Add. MSS., 35393, 16 Aug. 1802.
93 *Ibid.* 1 June, 26 Aug. 1802.
94 H. Cam, 'John Mortlock III, Master of the Town of Cambridge', *P.C.A.S.* Vol. XL (1939-42), pp. 2-10; *Camb. Chron.* 15 Oct. 1774, 9 Nov. 1776, 25 Mar. 1780, 15, 22 Feb. 1783.
95 *Camb. Int.* 28 May, 28 Nov. 1795, 22, 29 April 1797.
96 *Ibid.* 28 May 1795.
97 See B. Williams, 'The Eclipse of the Yorkes', *Transactions of the Royal Historical Society* 3rd Ser., vol II (1908); *Hardwicke Papers,* Add. MSS., 35393, 11 May 1802.
98 See *Hardwicke Papers,* Add. MSS., 35393 concerning 1802 election in Cambs.
99 *Camb. Int.* May, June, July 1802.
100 B. Flower, *An Address to the Freeholders of Cambridgeshire on the General Election* (1802).
101 *Ibid.* pp. 8-29; see also *Camb. Int.* 28 Nov. 1801.
102 *Hardwicke Papers,* Add. MSS., 35393, 25 May 1802.
103 *Ibid.* 10 May, 5 June 1802.
104 *Ibid.* 19 June 1802, 16 Aug. 1802.
105 Williams, 'Eclipse of the Yorkes', p. 50; *Camb. Chron.* 23 Mar. 1810.
106 Gray and Brittain, *Jesus College,* pp. 126-32; Knight, *University Rebel,* Chaps. 8-11.
107 *Camb. Int.* 7, 14 Dec. 1793
108 Winstanley, *Early Victorian Cambridge,* p.18.
109 Lincoln, *English Dissent,* pp. 246, 260-66.
110 *Ibid.* pp. 5-8; Adams, *Literary Backgrounds,* p. 18; *Camb. Int.* 29 July 1797.
111 Mineka, *Dissidence of Dissent,* p. 190.
112 Stromberg, *Religious Liberty,* pp. 37-39; Henriques, *Religious Toleration,* p. 32.
113 *Camb. Int.* 21 Feb. 1795. See also Flower, *National Sins Considered,* and B. Flower, *Divine Judgement on Guilty Nations; a discourse to Protestant Dissenters* (1804).
114 *Camb. Int.* 21 Dec. 1793.
115 *Ibid.* 24 Feb. 1798, 2 Mar. 1799, 26 July 1800.
116 *Ibid.* 4 June, 4 Jan. 1794, 4 Mar. 1797.
117 *Ibid.* 9 Jan. 1802.
118 Lincoln, *English Dissent,* p. 40; Cowherd, *Politics of Dissent,* p. 50.
119 Flower's *Political Review and Monthly Register* (Harlow, 1808), vol. III, Preface, xxxiv. See also vol. I, nos. III, pp.xlvi, xlvii; IV, pp. lix, lx.
120 *Camb. Int.* 15 Feb. 1794.
121 *Ibid.* 28 Sept. 1793, 27 Feb. 1796.
122 *Camb. Int.* 19 April 1794, 14 Oct. 1797.
123 *Ibid.* 21 April 1798, 21, 28 Sept., 30 Nov. 1799, 1 Aug. 1801.
124 *Ibid.* 26 Dec. 1801. See also 15 Feb. 1800, 9 Jan., 20, 27 Mar. 1802.
125 *Ibid.* 3 July 1802.
126 Lincoln, *English Dissent* 236-38; Henriques, *Religious Toleration,* p. 33.

127   H. Gow, *The Unitarians* (1928), p. 57.
128   *Camb. Int.* 19 Aug., 25 Nov. 1797.
129   *Camb. Int.* 22 April 1797.
130   *Ibid.* 26 Sept. 1795, 4 Feb. 1796, 13 May, 5, 19 Aug., 25 Nov. 1797, 12 May 1798
131   *Ibid.* 19 Aug., 22 April, 25 Nov. 1797, 12 May 1798.
132   *Ibid.* 7 April 1797.
133   *Camb. Int.* 2 June, 28 July 1798.
134   *Ibid.* 10 Nov. 1798. See also *Place Papers* B.M. Add. MSS. 27818 fol. 96.
135   *Ibid.* 9, 16 Feb. 1799.
136   *Ibid.* 14 Feb. 1801.
137   *Camb. Int.* 4 May 1799. See also Flower, *Proceedings of the House of Lords.*
138   *Address to the People of Great Britain* (1798).
139   I am grateful to E.P. Thompson for drawing this fact to my attention. See his 'Disenchantment or Default? A Lay Sermon', *in* C.C. O'Brien and W.D. Vanech (eds.), *Power and Consciousness* (1969), pp. 163-67.
140   *Camb. Chron.* 25 Mar. 1780, 15 June 1782.
141   *Camb. Int.* 20 April, 1799. Flower *Proceedings of the Lords,* p. xxv. While in prison Flower was visited by Henry Crabb Robinson - who had earlier contributed to the *Cambridge Intelligencer.* See *Diary, Reminiscences and Correspondence of Henry Crabb Robinson* ed. T. Sadler, I, (1872), p. 18.
142   *Camb. Int.* 18 June, 1803.
143   Thompson, 'Disenchantment or Default?', p.167.
144   *Camb. Int.* 26 Oct. 1799.
145   *Monthly Repository,* vol. V (1810), pp. 203-6.
146   *Camb. Int.* 18 Oct. 1800.
147   *Ibid.* 3 Jan. 1801.
148   *Ibid.* 10 Oct. 1801.
149   *Ibid.* 18 June 1803.
150   Flower, *Statement of the Facts,* p. xvii.
151   *Flower's Political Register,* Preface, vol. I (1807).
152   *Ibid.* Preface vol. I (1807).
153   *Place Papers* B.M. Add.MSS. 27818 fos. 64, 71, 96, 208, 244.
154   *Flower's Political Register,* vol. I, Jan. (1807), p. 1.
155   *Ibid.* Jan. 1807.
156   *Ibid.* II, July, p. vii; VI, Sept. p. lii; VII, Feb. p. xix; IX, Mar. p. xxiv.
157   *Ibid.* IV March, p. xlvi; IX, April, pp. xxxiii-xliv.
158   *Ibid.* II Aug., p. xxxi; III, Feb. p. xxxiv.
159   *Ibid.* IV, July, p. viii.
160   *Ibid.* VII, Feb., pp. xxi-xxviii.
161   *Ibid.* VII, Feb., pp. xviii-xx.
162   *Ibid.* vol. VII, April (1810), p. 328.
163   Eliza was a gifted composer and musician. The chief work of her musical life was the composition of *Hymns and Anthems* (1841). She composed several anthems to poetry written by her sister among them the well-known *Nearer, my God to Thee.* Mineka, *Dissidence of Dissent* pp. 190-198; S. Flower-Adams, *Vivia Perpetua* (1893), pp. v-xii.
164   Thompson, *Making of the English Working Class,* pp. 151, 179, 476, 726.

165 *The Cambridge Independent Press* 1819.
166 Thompson, *Making of the English Working Class,* p. 476; Read, *Press and People,* p. 75.
167 Thompson, *Making of the English Working Class,* pp. 151, 726.
168 Thompson, 'Disenchantment or Default?', *in* O'Brien and Vanech (eds.), *Power and Consciousness,* p. 166.
169 *Camb. Chron.* 16 Feb. 1793; *Cambridge Independent Press,* 5 Mar. 1825. (Hereafter abbreviated to *Camb. Ind. Press.*)
170 C. Humfrey, *A Report upon the present state of the River Cam with some suggestions* (1819).
171 H.C. Darby, *The Draining of the Fens* (1956 edn.) p. 123.
172 N. Kinderley, *The Ancient and Present State of the Navigation of the Towns of Lynn, Wisbech, Spalding and Boston* (1751).
173 Gooch, *General View of Agriculture,* pp. 211-12.
174 *Camb. Chron.* 23 Mar. 1793.
175 Gooch, *op. cit.* p. 223.
176 See Darby, *Draining of the Fens,* pp. 295-7.
177 S. Wells, *The History of the drainage of the Great Level of the Fens called the Bedford Level,* I, (1830), p. 756.
178 *The Inutility to the South Level of the intended new channel from Eau Brink to Lynn* (1793), p. 6.
179 Earl of Hardwicke, *Observations upon the Eau Brink Cut; with a proposal* (1793), pp. 2-15.
180 *Camb. Chron.* 5, 12 Oct. 1793.
181 N. Mutton, 'The Use of Steam Drainage in the Making of the Eau Brink Cut' in *Industrial Archaeology* 4, (1967), pp.353-57.
182 *Camb. Chron.* 11 May 1821.
183 *Ibid.* 27 Dec. 1822.
184 *Camb. Ind. Press* 5 Mar. 1825.
185 *Ibid.* 12 Mar. 1825; *Camb. Chron.* 11 Mar. 1825.
186 *Camb. Chron.* 17 June 1825.
187 *Ibid.* 1 June 1827, 12 Feb. 1830.
188 *Ibid.* 24 Aug. 1810.
189 *Ibid.* 15 June 1799, 11 May, 2 Nov. 1810.
190 *Ibid.* 5 Sept. 1781, 23 Nov. 1810, 18 June 1811. See also *Abstract of the Evidence given in support of the London and Cambridge Junction Canal Bill* (1812), pp. 20-23.
191 *Ibid.* 28 Sept., 23 Oct., 7 Dec. 1810, 15 April 1814.
192 *Ibid.* 21, 28 Dec. 1810, 12 April 1811.
193 *Ibid.* 6 Mar. 1812. See also 3, 17, 24 Sept. 1813, 8, 15 April 1814.
194 Gooch, *General View,* pp. 50, 51, 79, 95, 157, 239.
195 C.S. & C.S. Orwin, *The Open Fields* (1938), pp. 60, 65-66.
196 W.E. Tate, 'Cambridgeshire Field Systems' in *P.C.A.S.* XL (1944), p. 75.
197 *Camb. Chron.* 19 Sept. 1801.
198 *Ibid.* 15 Aug. 1795; Gooch, *General View,* pp. 60, 61, 70, 71, 84.
199 *Ibid.* 6 Dec. 1800.
200 *Camb. Chron.* 2, 31 May, 21 June, 18 July 1806; Cooper, *Annals* IV, p. 488.
201 Cooper, *Annals* IV, pp. 470, 637.
202 E. Jebb, *Cambridge: a brief study in social questions* (1906), pp. 19-20.

203   D. Fraser, *The Evolution of the British Welfare State* (1973), Ch. 2.

204   Hampson, *Poverty in Cambs.,* pp. 77-78, 246; *Report on the Charities of Cambridgeshire* VI, (1839), pp. 24-28; E. Stokes, 'Cambridge Parish Workhouses', in *P.C.A.S.* XV, (1910-11).

205   Stokes, *loc. cit.* pp. 113-16.

206   *Camb. Chron.* 24, 31 Jan., 25 July 1795, 20 Sept. 1800.

207   Hampson, *Poverty in Cambs.,* p. 193.

208   *Camb. Chron.* 22 Nov. 1800.

209   *Ibid.* 7 Nov. 1807; see also 22 Jan. 1819, 16 Oct. 1829.

210   Cooper, *Annals* IV, pp. 517-18.

211   *Camb. Chron.* 5 Jan. 1827. *Camb. Ind. Press* 17 May, 1828.

212   *Camb. Int.* 24 Jan. 1801.

213   *Camb. Chron.* 29 Oct. 1808.

214   *Ibid.* 5 Nov. 1808, 7 Jan. 1809.

215   *Ibid.* 20, 27 Feb., 6 Mar. 1818.

216   See T. McKeown and R. Brown, 'Reasons for the decline of mortality ... in the 19th century' in *Population Studies* (1962), 16, pt. 2.

3

Repression
and the Struggle for Reform
1815-1832

I

The fall of Napoleon and the restoration of the Bourbons was celebrated by a general illumination in Cambridge in 1814. The Corporation and University voted addresses to the Prince Regent congratulating him on the return to peace which was proclaimed with the accustomed solemnities. Marshal Blücher visited the University, and was drawn by the people of the town through the streets to Trinity College in triumphal procession. Later there was a great festival to mark the end of the war, and a general public dinner given by subscription on Parker's Piece.[1] Six thousand poor people managed to consume, among other things, over five thousand pounds of beef, seven hundred plum puddings and five thousand eight hundred penny loaves.[2] However, within months of Waterloo, the country was in the grip of a severe economic depression. Cambridgeshire shared with the rest of England the disastrous results of the Napoleonic Wars. The year 1815 brought depression to agricultural counties. During the war landlords had enclosed greedily, to take advantage of high prices, and had cultivated marginal lands that would pay to farm at these inflated prices but not at ordinary rates. Farmers also renewed their leases and invested capital in normally unproductive lands to meet the ever increasing wartime taxes and costs. Faced with falling prices and high interest charges, they were threatened with ruin after 1815.[3] Meetings were held all over the county to press Parliament to grant some measure of protection for agriculture and reduce the burdens of taxation. The government responded by passing the Corn Law of 1815 which prohibited the importation of wheat until the price in England reached 80/- a quarter. This was considerably higher than the average price and effectively prevented any imports except in years of very bad harvests.

Agricultural labourers were the first to suffer the contraction of land use after the Wars and distress was particularly acute in the Isle of Ely where scores of small farmers went bankrupt.[4] In May 1816 'a most desperate body of fen men' rioted at Littleport, marched to Ely, attacked several houses and extorted money.[5] After a few days of disorder there followed a further riot at Littleport in which two rioters were killed and seventy five taken prisoner and lodged in Ely gaol.[6] Five of the leaders were executed but the sporadic rioting continued, at Kirtling in 1822 and a similar disturbance at Sawston in 1823. These disturbances heralded the more widespread agricultural labourers' revolt of 1830.[7]

Though conditions improved in the 1820s agriculturalists still insisted that they could not 'compete upon equal terms with continental growers' and viewed 'with great alarm any alteration in the existing Corn Laws.'[8] Many feared that if the government were to be pressured by the middle classes into conceding reform of Parliament they would also 'sacrifice the interest of the Farmer to the cupidity of the Manufacturer.'[9]

The post-war political scene was equally disturbing. The atmosphere after Waterloo was one of alarm and suspicion, pretended conspiracies and genuine industrial unrest, especially in the Midlands and North. The cause of this distress and discontent, real and imagined, was to be found in the political and economic structure.[10] It led to an attempt on the life of the Prince Regent and thus gave the government an opportunity to react in a manner both prompt and severe. Reform was equated with revolution and there followed a period of government repression. This was the era of the suspension of *Habeas Corpus,* the Six Acts and Peterloo. Lord Liverpool's government viewed the situation with some trepidation and in Cambridge even the students' Union, which had continued to debate political issues, was suspended, and remained silent for the next four years.[11] Already burdened with these serious problems of agricultural distress and industrial unrest, to which few politicians could offer an effective solution, Parliament also had to deal with the continued demands for reform of the existing constitution, the currency system and the laws against Catholics.

Meanwhile, *The Cambridge Chronicle* was also going through a period of readjustment. James Hodson continued the policy of his father in almost every detail. His sales were still largely concentrated in the counties of Cambridge and Huntingdon, and the paper was also regularly filed at the 'Chapter and Peele's Coffee-Houses and at the Auction Mart' in London. It continued to be well supported in the county as regards advertisements and maintained its average of eighty or ninety per week from the area. The problem of bad debts remained and James, like his father, urged the public to pay promptly 'as the delay of prompt payments is, to the proprietor of a newspaper, to the full as formidable as the embargo was to this country.'[12] The free postal service for newspapers was as unreliable as ever, and newspapers and letters were often lost and occasionally tampered with − a situation about which the editor received 'numerous complaints'.[13] Most correspondents still asserted that the *Chronicle* was 'a valuable and widely circulated journal', and was also extensively read 'amongst the Members of the Senate, both within and out of the University'.[14] Though under a new editor, it made no attempt to appeal to a wider public. It was written for the conservative middle classes and members of the University, and remained ultra-Tory in outlook, advocating a largely negative, reactionary policy, taken mainly from the London Tory press.[15] It was a staunch advocate of the Anglican Establishment in England as well as of the Protestant ascendancy in Ireland. It strongly opposed Catholic emancipation and the reform of Parliament, and supported agriculture and the Corn Laws. It was completely out of sympathy with radical and working-class opinion in the town, and made little attempt to influence it in any way. Satisfied with its circulation figures and happy with the class that patronised it, Hodson did not consider editorials important, arguing that 'the upper classes use a Country Paper only for its local news and advertisements, and never dream of attending to the Editor's opinions.'[16] He accepted that 'there is a large class of their tenants and even their trades people who never see any other paper, and take their opinions from the County Journal.' However, to appeal to these lower classes was not the policy of the *Chronicle,* but of the radicals who 'know this well enough and have got hold of these journals to a great extent' in order to circulate their political views.[17] As regards borough corruption and Corporation jobbery in Cambridge, silence, rather than connivance, was his policy. This ultra-conservative outlook, plus the lack of any political comment and the pressure for reform in both the county and the borough, encouraged the founding of a rival newspaper in the town in May 1819, and the voice of liberal opposition, quiescent since the departure of Benjamin Flower in 1803, was raised again in Cambridge.

This paper, first established in Huntingdon in 1813 by Mrs. Elizabeth Carter Hatfield and entitled *The Huntingdon, Bedford and Peterborough Gazette and Northamptonshire General Advertiser,* was printed in Great New Street, London. Two years later it was being printed and published in Huntingdon, and Cambridge was now added to the title page.[18] The newspaper became finally established in Cambridge in May 1819 as *The Huntingdon, Bedford and Peterborough Gazette and Cambridge and Hertford Independent Press,* printed and published by Weston Hatfield, Market Hill, Cambridge.[19] It proved an immediate success, and quickly built up an extensive circulation. Hatfield was helped in the venture by his brother William, later to become proprietor of *The Northampton and Leamington Free Press.*[20] From its inception, therefore, it was very much a family concern, Weston's brother William, and his son James, also acting as agents.[21]

The format of the newspaper was not unlike that of the *Chronicle* which it challenged. It measured 22in x 15in and contained six columns on each of its four sides. The earliest numbers available had woodcuts of King's College Chapel and of Ely Catherdral on each side of the title. In Hatfield's own words, his newspaper contained 'interesting domestic occurrences of the week, Market tables, reports of County and Local Meetings on political and philanthropic subjects, copious Assize intelligence; parliamentary debates, original poetry, religious, political, agricultural and literary essays and foreign and national news.'[22] Agents were spread over the six adjoining counties, but its advertisements in 1830 indicate that its major area of circulation was confined to Cambridgeshire, Huntingdonshire and Bedfordshire.[23] By 1833 its circulation had reached a very respectable 1700. By 1840 this had increased to 2250 and the paper was liberally favoured with advertisements.[24] These rose from an average of approximately thirty per week in 1818 to sixty per week in 1825, and often reached as many as ninety in a single week.[25] One of the major reasons for Hatfield's success was his policy of publishing a column of political comment. This editorial expressed liberal principles and was devoted to the cause of popular progress. Hatfield soon became the 'representative of Reformers of his native and adjoining counties', and consistently voiced the opinions of the liberal element in town and University.[26]

The Cambridge Independent Press

He had the usual difficulties of an editor at the time, especially the problem of bad debts. By 1824 the newspaper was in debt for about £1500 because of persistent non-payment by readers, and as a result was 'on the point of sinking under an extent from the Crown', when a number of Whig noblemen and gentlemen from Cambridge and the surrounding counties came to the rescue, and advanced sums of money, on condition that control of the funds would be vested in Trustees. George Pryme, Fellow of Trinity and subsequently Whig M.P. for the borough, and Samuel Wells, the popular Huntingdon radical, were appointed and William Hatfield was also chosen to represent the family.[27] After the death of Weston Hatfield in 1837 there was an attempt by his daughters to recover part of the funds invested, and Pryme was accused of using the *Independent Press* not as a trustee 'but as a convenient vehicle for Mr. Pryme's politics . . . having helped to seat him for Cambridge.'[28] The editor of the rival *Chronicle* was also convinced that 'from first to last, the trusteeship in question has been simply a Whig-Radical effort for keeping Whiggery alive in this and the neighbouring counties.'[29] Nevertheless, assured of this financial backing, Hatfield was able to continue, and after his death the Trustees became the new registered proprietors.

When Hatfield first published *The Huntingdon Gazette* in 1813 'the liberties of Europe seemed fast withering in the grip of Napoleon' and he determined to bury 'every sense of private wrong and domestic grievance' until the war ended. However, now that *The Cambridge Independent Press* was firmly established, he felt free to comment on all matters as 'The necessity that previously imposed silence on the press, as it regarded matters of domestic polity, now no longer exists.'[30] Though Castlereagh 'designates as Jacobinical' everything that questioned government actions, Hatfield's aim remained 'the exposure and correction of the many abuses that exist both in and out of Parliament, to the subversion of the best interests of the public.'[31] This outspoken policy was not without its dangers in the years after 1815, and there were also major difficulties 'with which the friends of freedom in Cambridgeshire have to contend . . . All the influence of the Aristocracy, the Church, the Squirearchy, and of every class of corruptionist.'[32] He was aware 'that our increasing popularity has been regarded with a jealous eye from more quarters than one', but he refused to be intimidated, and was determined to continue to advocate 'Parliamentary reform, an alleviation of the public burden and a general amelioration of the conditions of the poor.'[33] Hatfield, like Flower, was to suffer for his liberal views, but he took pride in indicating that 'out of the six or eight prosecutions with which he had been assailed, not a single verdict had passed against him, at the hands of a British jury.'[34]

His policy could best be described as a mixture of Whig and radical ideas, similar to those advocated by Archibald Prentice in *The Manchester Times.*[35] In Hatfield's opinion the balance of the constitution had been upset. Corrupt interests had gained control in many boroughs besides Cambridge and Huntingdon, and the county representation was too often dominated by a noble family. Ministers of every government not only accepted the situation but actively encouraged it by lavishing offices and sinecures upon borough-mongers such as the Rutlands in Cambridge and their corrupt nominees. From the start, therefore, he attacked borough corruption in Cambridge and Huntingdon and supported the reform movement and its candidates in every election. Members of the Corporation 'whose gowns are a badge of disgrace' were responsible for 'a long list of charters violated, rights destroyed and charters abused.'[36] He advocated parliamentary and municipal reform and favoured the secret ballot, but rejected the radical scheme for universal suffrage and annual parliaments.[37] Hatfield denounced the government's attitude to the distress and discontent prevalent after 1815. He condemned the suspension of *Habeas Corpus* in 1817: 'For the mad acts of a few desperadoes, the whole people of England are libelled from the pulpit and disqualified from Parliament. The people require reform and retrenchment, and in return, they are deprived of the grand bulwark of their liberties.'[38] He was filled with outrage at the Peterloo massacre when 'scores . . . of unarmed English citizens [were] sabred in the streets of Manchester, when in the exercise of their undoubted constitutional rights.'[39] He warned the government that 'It is not spies, troops or executions that can obliterate discontent; the cause must be removed', and he suggested cutting taxation, retrenchment and an entire abolition of sinecures.[40] By 1820 he maintained that Lord Liverpool's government had been utterly discredited and that working-class loyalty had been confirmed. In his opinion the working classes should never have been 'identified with the deprived idlers of Spa-fields, the half starved blanketeers of Derby or the rash and headstrong peasants of Ely' but recognised as sensible and loyal subjects.[41] That they had remained so law-abiding when oppressed by Game Laws, the Six Acts and a savage Penal Code Hatfield considered marvellous.[42] However, the working classes were not the only sufferers. The 'distressed manufacturers of Manchester, of Leeds, of Birmingham and of Blackburn have no representatives in Parliament to state their grievances, to plead their wrongs and their misfortunes – and they hardly dare to meet to state their grievances, to consult on the best means of relief – the horrors of the 16th of August [Peterloo] are still vivid in their memory.'[43]

Though based in an agricultural region, Hatfield continually drew attention to the industrial North and its problems, and both accepted and preached the doctrine of Free Trade.[44] This meant he had to explain his policy on the contentious issue of the Corn Laws. He argued that they were oppressive, and would not really benefit the farmer whom they were designed to protect. He stated candidly: 'We are aware that our views on this subject may be somewhat unpopular among the class of society in which our paper perhaps most generally circulates, yet we will not, to gratify the present taste, or temporary interests of the farmer, give a sanction to the perpetuation of a system, which must ultimately prove destructive to their more permanent interests, while in the meantime it tends to degrade and pauperize the labourer.'[45] The burdens of the farmer, he accepted, must be eased, but agriculture must be protected not by a corn law but by a reduction of taxation, because he believed 'the state of the currency has a greater effect on influencing the price of corn (as indeed of almost every other article) than any legislative enactments, regarding the rate of imports.'[46] The farmer must therefore get his expenses reduced, especially the poor rate, and then by cutting his costs of production make more profit. The manufacturer should also share in the relief of taxation, thus enabling him to pay higher wages. He blamed most of the distress of the late 1820s on 'the growing scarcity of money' and insisted that this was the fault of the directors of the Bank of England, 'the unfeeling tyrants of the present day.'[47] Hatfield was convinced that the return to the gold standard after the Napoleonic War, which resulted in deflation, was a mistake for 'it cannot for a moment be denied, that paper currency gives a vast impetus to trade, and affords a field for enterprise and honourable speculation, which could not otherwise exist.'[48] Credit provided capital, and capital encouraged trade and employment, and so although there may be 'certain disadvantages in a paper currency, its benefits are manifold'. Correspondents warned him that because of his 'perpetual and determined hostility to the landed and agricultural interests, you shall . . . drive your readers belonging to those classes to abandon your paper', but he persisted in his belief that a reduction in taxation, and an expansion in the paper currency, were the solutions to the problem and denied that he was opposed to farmers: 'we never denied that the farmer was entitled to relief – we only differed as to the means.'[49]

At odds with the town and county over the great post-war issues of 'Cash and Corn', he also differed with them over the issue of Catholic emancipation. From the first the *Independent Press* was a staunchly nonconformist organ, the only one representing Dissent in the area. Like Flower twenty years earlier, Hatfield opposed the privileges of the Church of England and supported the demands of Dissenters and Roman Catholics for civil and religious equality. He therefore supported Daniel O'Connell, the leader of the emancipation movement in Ireland. The Catholic Association which he founded and the Catholic Rent which he collected he regarded as lawful, as 'its object is legitimate and praiseworthy, however unpalatable it may happen to be to those who are in power.'[50] He conceded that 'Mr. O'Connell, like Mr. Hunt, may have been more zealous than wise, but is that any reason why the people of Ireland are to be denied the possession of those rights, to which as British subjects, they are entitled? Emancipation he insisted was 'a civil right, not a religious one' and the Tory cry of 'No Popery' a bugbear, supported only by 'the clergy of the establishment . . . two or three contemptible corporations . . . and the Lords Mandeville and Manners; but surely the public will not be longer deluded by empty sounds.'[51] This was perhaps the major difference between the *Independent Press* and the *Chronicle.* Hatfield was prepared to be personal and controversial in his editorials, and he insisted that although the 'editor of a newspaper is at all times liable to the sneers and jeers, the ill and good will of the public . . . the duty of an editor of a public journal must be to give his opinion on all public questions.' One of his 'Constant Readers' praised this approach and stated that as a result of this policy a 'great portion of the town and county of Cambridge are indebted to you for much information, and bringing before the public many things which never would have appeared in *The Cambridge Chronicle.*'[52] Hatfield himself did not spare the *Chronicle:* 'our contemporary never gives a public opinion on any subject; least of all on one wherein we are concerned. At one time our contemporary avoided naming us lest he should bring us into public notice, but . . . if he really sought to promote truth, he would expose corruption, instead of flattering boroughmongers; if he really loved the cause of justice he would spurn at oppression, instead of seeking to perpetuate intolerance.'[53] Not surprisingly he admired Benjamin Flower and his controversial newspaper the *Intelligencer,* and all the more because 'Mr. Flower lived and wrote in stormy times, and once had his office windows saluted by a shower of stones from a church and king mob, led on by Pittite gownsmen and loyal cantabs, as the reward of his early Patriotism.'[54] Hatfield was determined to maintain Flower's aggressively liberal approach to national and local issues, and supported radicals and reformers in their efforts to alter the constitution in Church and State.

II

Events in the town and county during these years were to prove that reform was indeed the key to political change. In Leeds, Manchester and Birmingham the demand for parliamentary reform was associated with economic pressures for Free Trade and currency reform, and despite Hatfield's liberal advocacy of these measures in Cambridge the most powerful force in such older towns was the growing demand for a change in the structure of the old Corporation, often for both political and economic reasons.[55] In many places also these local attacks on the aristocracy, who happened to control boroughs, were made more fierce by nonconformist zeal.[56] The worst feature of the Cambridge Corporation from a local point of view was its political exclusiveness, as only supporters of the Duke of Rutland were allowed to join the ruling oligarchy. In a town of almost 20,000 inhabitants a mere 118 were resident freemen having the right to vote. After the death of Mortlock in 1816, the Rutland ascendancy in the borough of Cambridge was never again as powerful and, influenced by the growing movement for parliamentary reform, the townspeople grew more restive. They continued to pay rates and tolls and taxes but were still excluded from political power.

In 1818, stirred by William Whittred's *Letter to the Freemen,* which denounced the rule of Mortlock and his 'Chevely Clan', and supported by the *Independent Press,* they decided to contest the borough election for the first time since 1780.[57] Henry John Adeane opposed Generals Finch and Manners, the Rutland nominees.[58] He failed, and although the contest at this stage could be little more than a gesture of defiance, it prompted the Duke of Rutland to put forward 'a proposition for the admission of thirty-three inhabitants of the town to the freedom of the borough.'[59] A previous attempt to impose forty non-residents had been abandoned when opposed by Hatfield and other town reformers.[60] Hatfield saw the election as a turning point, as prior to this 'public opinion has been either stifled altogether or . . . its importance was unfelt and its consequences unknown. But a change for the better now begins. Men talk more freely as well as think more justly.'[61] These hopes of reform proved premature, for in the by-election which followed in 1819 only two freemen had enough courage to oppose Colonel Trench, 'the Rutland nominee from across the Irish Channel.'

However he was given a very hostile reception at the hustings, and en route to the Hoop Inn he was further assailed by 'cowardly radicals' who threw 'mud, old shoes, potatoes, stones and other missiles at him'. Later, an angry mob attacked the Hoop Inn where the Rutland followers were celebrating, 'demolishing the windows and casements', until at length the Riot Act was read and nine people were arrested, among them Weston Hatfield.[62] The trial gave Hatfield an opportunity to attack the Corporation in public, and he was defended by his ally, the liberal University Professor, George Pryme. Pryme maintained that the prosecution of Hatfield was a form of political persecution because 'the sentiments of my client have been published in his paper, and it is well known that his observations on all public proceedings and occurrences have been made in support of justice, liberty, social order and of all regular and lawful proceedings; although he may have attacked and reprobated the conduct and proceedings of other persons in the town and Corporation, whose conduct he, and almost every impartial man, considers to be reprehensible. This has drawn down upon him the decided enmity of those whom he has censured, and perhaps contributed to produce the prosecution.'[63] Hatfield also published his own version of his trial and acquittal, and cynically dedicated it to the Duke of Rutland, thereby giving himself a further opportunity to attack Rutland's corrupt domination of the borough.[64]

In 1820 Adeane was again requisitioned by the reform party to stand for election, accompanied on this occasion by George Pryme. A correspondent to the *Independent Press* welcomed this challenge to Rutland's power and maintained that the conduct of the Corporation, illustrated by 'the destruction or secretion of their books of orders, the violation of their known charters . . . their corrupt disposal of the prosperity of the Corporation,' was the real issue and ought to be publicly exposed.[65] The votes were two to one against Adeane and Pryme, which in the circumstances Pryme regarded as a result 'to excite gratification and triumph.'[66] The election was followed by a town meeting, despite the mayor's refusal to convene it, which appointed a committee to take steps to restore the rights and privileges of the unenfranchised townsmen, and addressed a petition to Parliament denouncing the state of the borough.[67] This was the first of a series of meetings in which town opinion, led by Pryme and aided by the *Independent Press,* expressed views hostile to the Corporation. Reform resolutions were carried, and petitions drafted in support of Queen Caroline (whom the King was now trying to divorce), the abolition of slavery and parliamentary reform.[68] Rutland, however, maintained his power until the passage of the Reform Bill, when the Corporation members were swept from power and Professor Pryme and Thomas Spring-Rice were elected as the new members for the town. Early in January of the year 1830 Hatfield and the reformers had invited Spring-Rice to stand for Cambridge. He had been at Trinity College before becoming M.P. for the City of Limerick, and had gained a reputation as a reformer and friend of civil and religious liberty.[69] Gunning had congratulated the newly enfranchised town on its independent choice. But the *Chronicle* did its best to stir up feelings against Spring-Rice, 'an Irishman, and personally an entire stranger to the electors', and recommended him 'to go back to Limerick where

Professor George Pryme

his merits will doubtless be better appreciated.' [70] Hatfield, on the other hand, condemned the policy of the Tory candidate, Sir Edward Sugden, in accepting the help of undergraduates in his canvass and also the interference of the Masters of Arts and Tutors of Colleges in the election.[71] The townspeople received 'the friend and supporter of Daniel O'Connell' with the most 'rapturous cheering and waving of hats', and subsequently voted him into second place. The disappointed editor of the *Chronicle* had to admit that the election result justified his worst fears, but expressed surprise at the size of Spring-Rice's majority.[72]

The townsmen during this period claimed one other notable and decisive victory, over the Tolls Case. The tolls in question were twopence on all carts laden with merchandise entering or leaving the borough of Cambridge. These tolls produced between four and seven hundred pounds per annum by 1827.[73] The imposition of this duty for an unlimited time and without parliamentary sanction was much resented by Cambridge tradesmen, and in 1824 they resolved to resist payment and a public subscription was launched to defray expenses. Hatfield again used all his literary skills in an effort to discredit both the Duke of Rutland and the Corporation. He printed bills for distribution and published his own report on the proceedings in 1826.[74] Rutland was denounced in the *Preface* for supporting a body that spent the toll money not on town improvements but wasted it in 'scenes of riot and gluttony' not to mention 'Feasts, monthly, annual and . . . on every occasion on which a pretext could be hung.' Furthermore to the Duke's utter discredit his 'liberality is the theme of their drunken boastings.'[75]

The Corporation duly brought an action for non-payment against three firms, the principal one being Messrs Samuel Beales, corn and coal merchants of Newnham. Beales claimed that the toll was not 'legalised either by usage or prescriptive right.'[76] The verdict was found for the defendants, but was suspended pending the result of another action against Fisher and Son, the Cambridge bankers. The Corporation claimed that if they should be deprived of the toll, which they had enjoyed for centuries, they would be sacrificing the greatest part of their corporate revenues.[77] The verdict this time was for the Corporation. A town meeting organised by the liberals decided 'to redouble the exertions to free themselves from the unjust and illegal exaction of Tolls'. Hatfield admonished the citizens for not contributing to the fund for expenses, and urged them to come to the support of 'the public spirited defendants' promptly, zealously, and cordially.[78] The action against Beales was tried again in December 1829, and the verdict given to the defendants and the town freed from this 'extremely vexatious and unjust' toll.[79] It was a major victory for the radical opponents of the Corporation and a public dinner was held at the Red Lion to celebrate the victory.[80] It was attended by the major reformers in the town. After the toasts had been given and the town and defendants congratulated on their stand against the tolls, Francis Gunning alluded to the value of a free press and free opinion. He referred to 'the vast and important change in public opinion in the town since the introduction of another vehicle for giving expression to it.' And with regard to the editor who had conducted that paper, 'he has done it with ability and a spirit of independence, that have been most serviceable to the cause.' He considered their thanks particularly due to Mr. Hatfield, 'who has ably and perseveringly drawn public attention to it, in the columns of his Journal, and who has materially aided it, by obtaining support from those, who would otherwise have been ignorant that their assistance was required.'[81] The subsequent loss of revenue proved calamitous for the Corporation. During the case they had been unable to exact the toll and the legal charges amounted to over five thousand pounds. The Rutland Club was irrevocably routed and disappeared amidst rejoicing from reformers.[82]

III

The county's history is somewhat different from that of the borough. Here elections were more open and there was a real possibility of effecting change. In in the 1820s Croker found national attention concentrated on what he called 'the three C's – Corn, Currency and Catholics'[83] but in Cambridge there is evidence of the continued importance of personal and local factors.[84] Parliamentary elections could still be largely determined by local loyalties, although national issues now began to play a larger part. The independent freeholders of the county, who had rejected C.P. Yorke in 1810 and put Francis Godolphin Osborne in his place, were determined to maintain the measure of independence they had gained. Charles Somerset Manners, the brother of the Duke of Rutland, realised that he would have to campaign vigorously if he hoped to retain his seat after 1815.[85] The county gentlemen resented his brother's monopoly of the borough, and these gentlemen opposed him in the county elections and constituted the nucleus of the so-called 'Independent Party'. Its organ was the *Independent Press*. Manners did, in fact, manage to retain his seat but he was forced to employ different tactics to those used by his brother in the borough. He had shown enthusiasm for local affairs and dispensed with any form of political pressure or intimidation. The county reform party, led by George Pryme, became particularly active after 1815. Meetings were frequently held in the years that followed and petitions drafted on agricultural distress and the other reform issues.[86]

'Cash, Corn and Catholics' were not, of course, the only issues, but they were central; they were all raised before 1815 and they continued to capture the attention of the country until 1846. Of the three the Catholic issue had most complicated the course of politics before 1815, but problems of cash and corn were also of importance, and as topics they were intimately interconnected in the eyes of most farmers. Corn prices, as already mentioned, continued to decline up to 1822, dropping to 43/- a qr. in that year. With prices so low there was no real question of an attack on the Corn Laws, but there was much talk of alleviating agricultural distress by cutting taxation. Not all the country gentlemen understood the economic arguments of Ricardo, but Hatfield did endeavour to make them realise, through his editorial comment, that the debate was about fundamental questions such as the place of agriculture in society, the relationship between consumers and producers, the composition of Parliament, the competing claims of landlords and industrialists and the proper role of government. These subjects captured the attention of Whigs, Tories and Radicals, and they were all openly debated in county election meetings in the 1820s. These meetings were attended not only by Osborne, Pryme, Gunning and the county reform group, but also by radicals such as Samuel Wells, members of the University and titled 'outsiders' such as the Duke of Bedford, Earl Fitzwilliam and Lord Dacre.

To the radicals parliamentary reform was the question of the hour and was seen as an indispensable preliminary to all other reforms. The Tories maintained that whatever reform was introduced should be almost imperceptible in its operation. Gunning put the Whig case for the 'Independent Party', rejecting universal suffrage — a measure which he believed would lead to revolution. However, without the introduction of some element of moderate reform, he insisted 'revolution would sooner or later be the case.'[87] The editor of the *Chronicle* did not openly oppose reform but enjoyed the discomfiture of the Whigs when their radical allies gained control of a well attended meeting in 1823 and demanded universal suffrage, annual parliaments, an end to Crown lands and tithes and the disestablishment of the Anglican Church. These views provoked jeering from gownsmen who were present, which in turn excited the 'lower orders', and a riot ensued. Gunning and the Whigs, who had often complained of University interference at these meetings, were shaken by the behaviour of their allies and more so when Samuel Wells accused them of being 'greater enemies to reform than the Tories.' In his opinion 'Whig and Tory were the two thieves between which the constitution had been crucified.' Hodson took pleasure in pointing out to the Whigs that their fickle allies, whenever it suited their purposes, could 'successfully turn the tide of public opinion against them, and completely vanquish them, on their own ground.'[88] Nevertheless he was utterly opposed to the teachings of those Cobbett-inspired 'factious itinerant orators' who wanted to reform Parliament so that they could 'defraud the fundholder and plunder the Church.'[89]

Despite these events at county meetings, for much of the 1820s Catholic emancipation was the most pressing political problem, completely overshadowing even parliamentary reform.[90] It had been a problem since the Act of Union with Ireland in 1800, but after 1820 the crises became more frequent and intense. The divisions in the Tory party in these years were not due to parliamentary reform, but to corn and Catholics. The Catholic question on which they had agreed to differ in 1812 was still demanding a solution, and from a party point of view was more serious because on this issue the Whigs were united. The bills submitted to Parliament in 1819 and 1821 showed that increasing numbers of younger members favoured emancipation. When O'Connell captured the loyalty of the Irish peasantry and founded the Catholic Association in 1823, religious differences became hopelessly bound up with national feelings and the land war in Ireland. Soon, the solution to the question was being accepted by politicians as a matter of political necessity, not of religious toleration. This was the policy adopted by Hatfield in his editorials.[91] Nevertheless, in centres such as Cambridge there was a new stirring of 'No Popery' passions in the 1820s. Here was an issue where town and county politics became entangled.

As we have already seen the Cambridge Corporation was a traditional Tory body with a strong devotion to the establishment, epitomised by Colonel Trench's pledge after the election of 1819 to be the enemy of 'Jacobinism, Atheism and Anarchy.'[92] Ostensibly the real issue at stake in these years in the borough was whether the House of Rutland was to be allowed to maintain its hold on the town. Its power was menaced by the growing reformist element, pursuing Benthamite ideas, which, led by Pryme and supported by Hatfield, was able to thrive among a certain intelligent educated class in the town and University. This same group often supported the attack on the established Church by pressing for Catholic emancipation, which was also seen as an indirect attack on the powers and privileges of the Corporation. The University and Corporation were correct in realising that the supporters of emancipation would later be the promoters of schemes for municipal and Church reform. They were only too well aware of the determined dissenting element involved, and feared therefore for the established Church. They continued to petition Parliament against the Catholic claims,[93] and in the 1820s the 'No Popery' issue was to provide a very suitable rallying cry for Tory votes in town and University. The *Chronicle* shared this outlook, and lent its support to the Tory cause. The threat to the established Church was powerful enough to occasion, in 1825, the founding of a new newspaper to defend the Tory position. This was *The Huntingdon, Bedford and Cambridge Weekly Journal*, owned by H.G. James and 'Printed and Published for the Proprietor by A.P. WOOD', at the Journal office in Huntingdon.[94]

This paper was set up to rival the growing influence of the *Independent Press* but survived only until 1828. Its opening editorial stressed that it was not founded 'from sordid or mercenary motives' but to fill a definite need. Of *The Cambridge Chronicle* it was 'unwilling to speak in any terms but those of respect, but its columns are closed against being made the arena of political discussion', and this was a decided disadvantage for the Tory cause in the area at such an important time. It declared quite openly that it was the unconstitutional sentiments and radicalism of the *Independent Press* 'that first prompted the present undertaking', and while its radicalism made it palatable only to a few, 'the circumstances of its being the only political Paper in this quarter, has given it an ascendancy which it could not have otherwise obtained.'[95] The first editorial set the tone of the newspaper for the next four years. It condemned Samuel Wells as capable of seeing only with 'the aid of Cobbett's spectacles' and denounced the radicalism he 'mistakenly' advocated. However it regarded Catholic emancipation as a much more serious menace, because 'we can prove that the spread of the Catholic Faith has uniformly been accompanied with political tyranny and mental darkness; that a good Catholic cannot be a good servant of the public, because he owes a higher obedience to the ecclesiastical than to the civil power'. Furthermore, the Catholic clergy were 'a body of men who have always prostituted their authority to purposes of tyranny and oppression.'[96] This was a theme it returned to over and over again during the course of the struggle for emancipation.[97] O'Connell was 'the Irish Gracchus', always willing to descend to 'personal abuse, self adulation and vicious oratory',[98] and only happy when 'wallowing in his native element of rancorous hostility to England.'[99] The remedy for Ireland's 'ignorant, degraded, oppressed' people was not Catholic emancipation but 'the disenfranchisement of the forty shilling freeholders', emigration, improving landlords and a policy of improvement and alteration for the Irish village which would cause it to resemble its English counterpart.[100] Weston Hatfield with his 'foul-mouthed, slanderous imputations on the public authorities' was seldom spared, nor were the new workers' combinations in the North, or slave traders.[101] Besides giving its full support to the government, it favoured the agricultural interest and the Corn Laws in a modified form, freer trade, emigration, the National Debt and the local Corporations, especially in their stand against Catholic emancipation.[102]

The *Journal* was not a success. Despite its Tory sentiments its advertisements, which were never numerous, declined rapidly over the four years. The first two years saw it averaging twenty advertisements per week, but this quickly declined to a mere ten advertisements per week in the final two years of its existence. An early union with 'a Newspaper about to be established in Northamptonshire', and an attempt to concentrate on that county denied it any substantial chance of success in Cambridge, where it came to rely on the *Chronicle* for most of its local news.[103]

However, aided by these two newspapers, Tories in the area were to make a determined stand against further concessions to Catholics. The issue became a particularly vital one in University elections in the twenties, splitting the Whig and Tory parties and causing great excitement in the town. In 1822 the Tory candidate, W.J. Bankes, denounced emancipation and emerged victorious.[104] The *Chronicle* continued to support the cause of the established Church with brief editorials in the years that followed, and occasionally buttressed these with extracts from the London Tory press and various magazines.[105] Meanwhile, the *Independent Press* advocated emancipation and printed many letters in its favour, arguing that it would be just, wise, liberal and tolerant to grant the measure.[106] Extremist opinions on both sides reached their height in the general election of 1826 which was fought with unexpected eagerness all over the country.[107] Among the topics in the election were economic retrenchment, parliamentary reform and abolition of slavery, but the main issue in Cambridge, as elsewhere, was Catholic emancipation and, to a lesser extent, the Corn Laws. At the borough hustings Pryme admitted that there was no reasonable prospect of success, but openly advocated Catholic emancipation and Free Trade.[108] Colonel Trench, on the other hand, denounced Catholics 'whose object appeared to be, by the attainment of political power, to put down the Protestant Establishment and advance their own'. These sentiments were greeted with 'immense cheers'. Pryme managed to obtain only four votes and a disgruntled Hatfield dismissed the election as 'a farce.'[109]

In the county election *The Times* maintained that the proceedings were so dull that it 'hardly deserves the name of a contested election.'[110] The main interest was provided by the decision of the Cambridge-based 'Independent Party' to contest the county seats. This was unusual, as urban leaders rarely interfered in county affairs. They nominated Adeane as a third candidate, but being personally pledged to Osborne he had no wish to stand.[111] His supporters were not deterred but Manners and Osborne were returned. The real struggle developed in the University election, a fact reflected in the local press from January 1826 onwards. In the columns of the *Chronicle* letters debated the candidates suitability, the fairness of election expenses and the justice of Catholic claims.[112] Viscount Palmerston, a University representative since 1811, was opposed by two of his colleagues in the government, J.S. Copley (the Attorney-General) and Henry Goulburn, as well as by W. Bankes the member elected in 1822. The fact that Palmerston was the only pro-Catholic of the four, in the words of the *Chronicle,* 'renders the contest somewhat peculiar.'[113] His colleagues could arouse opposition to him on the grounds that he was a pro-Catholic and, furthermore, he could not count on government patronage. Deserted by the government, Palmerston suffered the disadvantage of being a pro-Catholic in the face of preponderant anti-Catholic feeling in the University.[114] However, as the editor of the *Chronicle* indicated, despite being a Tory he could at least 'reckon upon the votes of many of the Whigs' because of his Catholic sympathy.[115] The Whigs both within and outside the University proved enthusiastic in Palmerston's cause, but he remained apprehensive because 'the great majority of the Electors are rural Reverends', and opinion in the *Chronicle* during these weeks was against him.[116] However, in the poll he was returned second to Copley and his success was regarded as a triumph by the pro-Catholics, just as Copley's was by the anti-Catholics. The support given to Palmerston by the Whigs encouraged him to accept office in Lord Grey's government in 1830.[117]

By now emancipation had also become the key issue in the Cambridge Union, where it was fiercely debated in front of opposing undergraduate factions.[118] Meanwhile, the *Chronicle,* and the majority of the electors in Cambridge, continued to suspect the campaign for Catholic emancipation as being no more than a cloak for more insidious designs.[119] Fears were reawakened when the more liberal Canning became Prime Minister in 1827. When Burdett's motion in favour of emancipation was passed the following year, Hatfield concluded that it 'is now clearly the wish of the nation at large that these civil distinctions on account of differential points of faith should cease.'[120] With the success of O'Connell at the Clare by-election in 1828 he claimed that peace could now only be secured by concession, and by the end of the year he was convinced that even as staunch a Tory as Peel had accepted the necessity of such action.[121] The *Chronicle* was now reduced to dependence on the House of Lords to prevent 'the granting of political power to papists.'[122] During the passage of the bill on Roman Catholic Relief through Parliament in the early months of 1829, the final stronghold was breached when an anti-Catholic petition was defeated in the University Senate by eight votes due, according to the *Chronicle,* to the 'somewhat unexpected arrival of several members of the Inns of Court, who came down for the express purpose of voting upon this occasion.'[123] Hatfield contended, however, that even without these arrivals the vote would have been lost, and asked why no comment was made by the *Chronicle* on the 'expected arrivals' from Ely.[124] Letters and petitions proved of no avail.[125] At a final meeting in the Shire Hall convened by the Mayor, the Rev. Chevallier now accepted that the question was no longer one of religious toleration but 'one of a political nature', and Mr. Fawcett added that the country had been 'belied, betrayed and ruined by its Parliament . . . [and] the petitions of the people . . . thrown back to them as trash.' The voices of Henry Gunning and other reformers were drowned amidst 'tremendous uproar' when they tried to negative the anti-Catholic petition and the original petition was carried 'amidst deafening shouts of applause.'[126] Catholic emancipation had arrived but toleration, it appears, had not. Relief in Ireland was only granted along with disenfranchisement. Tolerant conviction played no part in either the Government's purpose or the people's acceptance. In Cambridge there must have been many who sympathised with the eccentric vicar of Kingston, the Reverend Maberly, who refused to accept the *fait accompli* and continued to disturb county meetings with speeches concerning the Catholic menace,[127] and though the excitement had abated in the town, it was still possible 'here and there to see inscribed upon the walls "No Popery . . ."[128]

A View in Sidney Street Cambridge 1830

IV

Despite the more liberal tone of Lord Liverpool's government after 1822, evidenced particularly in the movement towards freer trade introduced by Huskisson, the provincial demand for parliamentary reform remained as strong as ever. Attempts had been made by Lord John Russell and others to effect piecemeal reform, but these had also been rejected, showing how serious a cleavage had grown up between opinion in the landlord-dominated Parliament and that of the middle classes, particularly in the industrial provinces.[129] Hatfield was not impressed by the record of the Tories and urged the people not 'to rest contented with the little that had been ceded to them', nor to place 'too blind a confidence in the supposed liberality of the present administration', but to continue the struggle for reform.[130] The return of agricultural and industrial depression in 1829 gave fresh impetus to the national movement. The reform group in Cambridge had gone from strength to strength and was now supported, often vociferously, at many of its meetings by the working-classes who, according to the *Chronicle,* 'for want of other employment, took an active part' in carrying proposed resolutions.[131] Hatfield defended their right to attend, stressing that their presence 'tended to demonstrate that every class of people was alive to the distress which exists', and that under such pressure reform was inevitable.[132]

At one such county meeting in January 1830 Adeane spoke about agricultural distress, and petitions to Parliament were organised demanding the total repeal of the duties on malt and beer. Consequently in the county election of that year Adeane was asked to stand in opposition to Manners. The reformers' prospects of success seemed good, as both Osborne and Adeane were popular local men 'holding opinions favourable to civil liberty' and reform, and the *Chronicle* accepted that 'an arduous contest appears inevitable.'[133] The Tories expected Manners to be returned but against a background of agricultural distress and depression in the county, the reformers had their best opportunity to date for effecting change. Every resident freeholder in the county was personally solicited by both parties. The town during election week 'exhibited a scene of the most animating description, the streets being enlivened by bands of music, and the display of various elegant banners etc.'[134] The election had captured wide public interest and it was significant that at the hustings on Parker's Piece Manners faced loud disapprobation, whereas Osborne and Adeane were received 'with loud and long continued cheering.'[135] Both proceeded to speak in favour of the Corn Laws and parliamentary reform, but Manners would not commit himself to the latter. By the end of the week he was forced to admit defeat, and left town before the final result was announced. Adeane and Osborne were chaired 'amidst enthusiastic cheers of the numerous assemblage' and Pryme congratulated the freeholders on achieving the culmination of work begun in 1810.[136] A disappointed editor of the *Chronicle* was forced to state that 'The Result was to us, we candidly admit, quite unexpected', and ample proof that a considerable change has taken place in the political opinions of the freeholders . . . 'the return of two Whig Members being decisive of the fact.'[137] Hatfield was delighted that the people had finally 'acted for themselves and vindicated their rights', and now looked forward to a period of reform under the Whigs.[138]

The return of the Whigs to power in 1830 made it certain that some sort of reform bill was inevitable; it was not certain, however, what form the bill would take. Henry Brougham and Lord John Russell were the two most likely politicians to decide the content as the Prime Minister, Lord Grey, had no specific plan for reform. The Whigs, exclusive and aristocratic as they were in their attitude to government, were ready to accept political innovations.[139] They believed that unless reform was accomplished quickly, more dangerous forces would effect more uncontrollable innovation. Also, unless this measure was considerable enough to assuage discontent, it would be of little use. Both the major parties accepted that democracy was unpalatable, and radical ideas dangerous. Political power should only be granted to those with a certain amount of property so that social stability could be guaranteed. Nevertheless, Russell's first bill in March 1831 went much further than most politicians anticipated. The *Chronicle* declared that 'The most ardent advocates of reform . . . took no pains to conceal their astonishment with what they saw introduced . . . a proposal, which in the violence of its changes, and the sweeping character of its enactments more than realised their utmost hopes.'[140] Hatfield was enthusiastic about the bill, 'great and grand in every sense', and openly campaigned for its acceptance.[141] Small boroughs of less than two thousand inhabitants were to be completely disenfranchised and those with a population of less than four thousand were to lose one of their two M.P.'s. The seats created were to be given to the big new towns and the counties. As to the franchise, in the counties the right to vote was confined to the forty shilling freeholders, but in the boroughs the vote was to be offered to the £10 householder, the man who occupied buildings of an annual value of £10. The *Chronicle* stated unequivocally that the bill amounted to a revolution. It was now publishing much more powerfully-worded editorials, and this was probably the result of the death of James Hodson in February 1832 'after a protracted illness',[142] which gave his son Francis Hodson and his new partner Charles Edward Brown, the opportunity to take over the paper.[143] Brown's father had been postmaster in Green Street for many years, and had also been a printer for the Hodsons since they had taken over the *Chronicle*. He eventually acquired an interest in the concern, and his son Charles was introduced to the business in the 1820s and worked for Hodson – mainly as a bookkeeper – until James Hodson's death in 1832.[144] The two young editors confirmed that they would maintain the principles upon which the newspaper was founded, supporting the established Church and the constitution, and they expressed their determination to oppose 'the rash innovators [who] now threaten it.'[145] For the first time in the history of the *Chronicle,* now established for almost seventy years, a weekly editorial began to appear, with opinions on political events. It became the mouthpiece of the anti-reform element in the town and University and throughout the reform crisis of 1831-32 it opposed the reform fever which now raged more strongly than ever in the county.

Meetings in favour of the Reform Bill were held and reformers were agreed that 'the proposed bill went to every possible extent they could wish', and urged the electors of Cambridge to demand 'the bill, the whole bill, and nothing but the bill', because 'the cry against reform was almost confined to the borough-mongers.'[146] In the elections that followed in May 1831 Manners supported by 'the Yorke and Peyton interests', was reputed to be making an effort to regain his seat in the county. But he retired from the contest before the poll, realising that he had little hope of success, and the two reformers Adeane and Osborne were returned unopposed.[147] The University contest excited far more interest but the reformers Palmerston and Cavendish were defeated. The editors of the *Chronicle* saw their rejection as 'proof of the way in which the Reform Bill is regarded by the educated class' and insisted that their defeat was 'not just an act of the Clergy', as implied by the London newspapers.[148] However, the *Independent Press* was in no doubt as to the general feelings of the people of Cambridge on the matter, Cavendish's carriage being drawn out of town by the townspeople.[149] In October Osborne resigned, and in his farewell speech wrote: 'I found the representation in the hands of two great families, whose influence was predominant; I leave it where it ought to be, in the free and un-influenced possession of the Freeholders of the County', and at the subsequent by-election they easily defeated a combined attempt by the 'two great families' to regain the seat for Captain Yorke, electing instead another Whig reformer, Richard Greaves Townley of Fulbourn, the nominee of Lord John Russell.[150]

The editors of the *Chronicle* were undaunted by these events and continued their attacks on the Reform Bill and its supporters in the local and national press, in particular *The Times* and *The Morning Chronicle*.[151] They disagreed with the arbitrary nature of disenfranchisement, and with boroughs losing their seats 'not because they were corrupt' but because they had less than two thousand or four thousand voters.[152] They insisted that the new system was being rushed through Parliament, while every 'fresh enquiry lays open some new and gross defect', so that the reformed system would emerge just as corrupt and full of anomalies as its predecessor.[153] Influence, they argued, would inevitably pass from the landed to the industrial areas and would mean the eventual destruction of the Corn Laws because the new House of Commons would be far too dependent on town votes and would only be able to exist 'by a tame a servile compliance with the manufacturers' cry of Cheap Bread.'[154] Despite Whig denials the bill would merely be a prelude to 'a total subversion of the British Constitution.' Furthermore, it would be politically naive to expect that these 'revolutionary measures can be stopped, just at the point which their advocates choose.'[155] However, the major concern of both editors, and the numerous correspondents, was the extension of democracy accomplished by the £10 household franchise. They insisted that the consequent pressure on the House of Commons would make it very difficult to carry out the King's government effectively. This extension of the franchise could hardly be accepted by editors who believed that one of the numerous fallacies at the time was 'that the middling classes are now so well informed in this country that they ought to have a greater share in the Government.'[156] The £10 clause was regarded as 'one of the most dangerous innovations – by many who supported the general principle of reform.'[157] They found it difficult to accept the fact that 'any man paying for his house the weekly rent of 3s. 10¼d., will have as great a share in the return of a member of Parliament as a man of £10,000 a year', and stated there was 'but a step from this point to universal suffrage.'[158]

The *Independent Press* welcomed the bill but adopted the radical view that the bill itself was not important – it was merely a means to an end. It could not be regarded as a panacea for political and economic ills, and Hatfield cautioned the working classes not to expect too much from it.[159] As a first stage it was enough; the principle of reform had been accepted and the power of the Corporation in the town and the aristocracy in the county was threatened by its acceptance. Hatfield was, however, disappointed that the government had not seen fit to introduce the secret ballot, and condemned the Chandos clause (which gave the county vote to tenant farmers who held land at a rent of not less than £50 a year) as 'not in keeping with the spirit of the Bill.'[160] The bill itself was only acceptable as a temporary measure, and he hoped it would be speedily consolidated by other reforms from the new ministry. His cautious optimism was vindicated in the new elections of December 1832. Pryme and Spring-Rice were returned for the borough, but in the county election Captain Yorke headed the poll, with the Whigs Townley and Childers (nominated by the 'Independent Party') second and third, Adeane losing his seat. These events convinced Hatfield of the necessity for more reform, as he felt the Tory success in the county was due to the divisions that existed among the liberals and the landowners' influence over the new £50 'Chandos elector', an influence which, he maintained, could only be broken by the introduction of the secret ballot.[161] Satisfied with their control of the borough Pryme and the 'Independent Party' appeared to lose interest in county politics which quickly slipped back under Tory control.[162]

V

Between 1831 and 1851 the population of Cambridge increased from 20,917 to 27,803.[163] This rate of increase, though not as great as in other parts of England, was remarkable for a university town. The Municipal Corporations Act of 1835 dissolved the old oligarchic corporation but the newly elected Council seemed equally unable to cope with the many problems of a growing urban society. Lack of funds, administrative drive and the permissive nature of the act prevented the introduction of any significant improvements. One correspondent commented that after decades of talk about improvement the streets were still 'in a most disgraceful and dangerous state and the proper authorities do not seem inclined to stir in the matter.'[164] In 1849 the exasperated editor of the *Chronicle* stated that because of this lethargy Cambridge had been 'outstripped in the march of improvement by places of far inferior note and means.'[165] Before the dissolution of the old Corporation gas street lighting had been introduced and new sites found for the Cattle and Corn Markets, though they were criticised as 'the most inconvenient that could have been chosen.'[166] In 1842 a new Shire House was built but to make way for it the old Norman gatehouse was demolished—a measure, according to the *Cambridge Guide* of 1868, that could only be described as 'a ruthless piece of vandalism.'[167] The disastrous fire of 1849 gave the town a market-place more in keeping with the volume of local trade. The original market was little more than a wide street but the destruction of eight houses on the night of September 15 gave the Town Council the opportunity to rebuild and the result was the present market square, opened in the early fifties.[168]

The editor of the *Chronicle* led the campaign for a new cemetery and informed his readers that town churchyards were 'packed and crammed to a degree which renders them disgusting to the sense and dangerous to public health.'[169] After some sustained pressure Cambridge became one of the first towns to open new cemeteries outside its city boundaries, the first near Histon Road (1842) and later another near Mill Road (1848).[170] Under the terms of the Public Health Act of 1848 ratepayers got a Local Board of Health but the *Chronicle* argued that it proposed 'too much interference with everything and everybody.' Despite the unsatisfactory performance of the local council in health matters the editor objected strongly to 'the centralising principle.'[171] *The Cambridge Advertiser* on the other hand wholeheartedly welcomed any development which would help conquer 'the vested interests of filth and plague.'[172]

In Cambridge as elsewhere there was little provision for working-class education in the first half of the nineteenth century.[173] In the eighteenth century the Dame and Charity schools did what they could to teach the three R's and were helped in the 1790s by the foundation of the Sunday School movement, and by 1834 nearly all the parishes in the town had at least one school.[174] However most of these efforts were concerned not with refashioning the way of life of the poor but with keeping them in their due place in society by instruction in the scriptures and in catechism. Nevertheless, scores of pamphlets were written warning of the danger of education exalting the poor above their humble and laborious duties.[175] The main obstacle, however, to the development of an educational system in Cambridge and elsewhere, was the religious zeal of the sponsors of the voluntary societies and the struggle that followed between Anglicans, who demanded complete control, and Nonconformists, who emphasised religious liberty.[176] In Cambridge the Anglican National Society, liberally supported by the University, controlled what education system existed and opposed any state interference in the 1830s.[177] The *Independent Press* advocated a non-sectarian, national scheme for education and supported the Whig non-denominational education clauses of the Factory Bill of 1839. The *Advertiser* also gave its support and asserted 'that in no place, equal in extent and population, is the education of the poor less cared for, than in Cambridge. In no place is ignorance so prevalent, or its attendant vices, idleness and profligacy, more abundant.'[178] Despite the building of some additional schools in the town the total number of children attending elementary and other schools remained depressingly low.[179]

In the county there was continued depression in agriculture until the 1840s and the process of mechanisation and improvement remained slow. The period between 1815 and 1850 was therefore one of the worst periods of existence for the agricultural labourer and made the agricultural labourers' revolt of 1830 inevitable.[180] Cambridgeshire, with eleven per cent of the population in receipt of Poor Relief, had its share of arson, wage riots and machine breaking. A.J. Peacock, who has published an authoritative study of these events, concludes that 'the tyranny of the countryside was a very real thing during this period.'[181] High wages were often paid to agricultural labourers as a sort of insurance against violence and arson. It is against this background that one must set the farmers' determination to maintain the Corn Laws and the agricultural labourers' resistance to the Poor Law of 1834.[182] Some progress was recorded in the 1840s and many looked forward to further improvements when Cambridgeshire became linked to London by rail, but James Caird in 1850 records the continuation of social unrest and a consequent reluctance on the part of farmers to invest in labour-saving machinery.[183]

The coming of the railways did much to reaffirm the general belief in the possibilities of improvement and produced in East Anglia for the first time a familiarity with power-driven machines, and a sense that these machines might be something more than just socially-embarrassing instruments of industrial competition. They influenced, directly or indirectly, the development of most industries in England, but agriculture was affected hardly less than manufactures. In the long run, the growth of a national newspaper system and a daily post, as well as the opportunity of cheaper travel, helped to unify England in a way that hitherto had not been possible.[184]

To many people Cambridge was the natural gateway to the eastern counties and, having established itself as the main river port and market in the county, was an obvious focal point for railway promotion, quite apart from its possible significance as an intermediate stage to the North.[185] Proposals in the early twenties, such as those by William James for a link between Bishop's Stortford and Clayhithe sluice, and John and George Rennie, for a line from London Bridge to Cambridge, proved unsuccessful.[186] However, a survey by James Walker in 1835 met with some parliamentary success. This was for a line from London to Cambridge via Broxbourne and Bishop's Stortford.[187] Lack of capital prevented the new Company, the Northern and Eastern, from building its line as far as Cambridge and, having reached Bishop's Stortford in 1842, it was terminated, at least for the time being. The Company had intended to make Cambridge a railway centre but local opposition from landowners and the University prevented the building of projected lines to Bedford, Oxford and York.[188] A well attended meeting in 1834 had listened attentively while Mr. Cundy, the civil engineer, spoke of the advantages a rail link with London would bring, particularly stressing the enormous benefit of 'conveyance for agricultural and manufacturing produce, and the extension of manual labour.'[189] It would open up the London market, especially for livestock sales, thereby helping to alleviate agricultural distress. It would also make Cambridge an excursion centre, which would give a welcome stimulus to local trade.

Letters to the newspapers endorsed his views but some disapproved because of the cost involved, while others were apprehensive about the decline of horse-breeding and horse sales, not to mention the possible disfigurement caused to agricultural land and the opportunities offered for ruinous speculation.[190] George Pryme, the Whig M.P., was reluctant to get involved in the debate because many principal inhabitants of Cambridge were averse to the scheme. The newspaper editors were in favour of railways, though they had certain reservations. The *Independent Press* accepted that some unwelcome changes might have to be accepted as the price of progress, but 'we have not the slightest apprehension respecting the soundness of the railroad principle.'[191] The *Chronicle* favoured the town as a centre for railways, for to be without them would be 'the most tantalizing and annoying position in which a provincial town can be placed in these days of steam and iron.'[192] The *Advertiser* agreed: 'Not to have a railway is now to be out of this world' and condemned the attitude of Cambridge people who had 'hitherto displayed an apathy which is as extraordinary as it is discreditable.'[193] Though showing some hostility to most other schemes, the University and the landed proprietors were in favour of the Northern and Eastern Company's proposal and were able to wring important concessions from the Company when the line eventually reached the town.

Two factors stimulated new developments in 1843. The first was an improvement in the affairs of the Northern and Eastern Company, which was amalgamated with the Eastern Counties Railway. This encouraged it to get parliamentary permission to complete the line to Cambridge. Secondly, a proposed extension of the London and Birmingham line to Peterborough, making the latter the centre of an eastern railway network, provoked a certain amount of consternation in the town.[194] A further threat appeared in 1844 with the proposal for a railroad from London to York which would bypass Cambridge altogether and 'instead of making it the central point from which various lines would branch out' would isolate it and thus prove to be 'highly detrimental to the interest of the town.'[195] Public meetings were quickly held and the *Chronicle* urged the townspeople to get rid of their 'habitual apathy' by supporting the alternative London to York proposal which was routed to pass through both Cambridge and Lincoln.[196] This proved unsuccessful, but the disappointment was mitigated by the opening of the London to Cambridge line on July 29, 1845 'with every possible degree of éclat.'[197]

The editorial in the *Chronicle* claimed that Cambridge travelling had undergone a revolution. The four horse coach had been forced 'to succumb to the irresistible march of steam.'[197] The University authorities were more apprehensive about the effect the new railway would have on their undergraduates and wrung certain concessions from the railway Company. The station was exiled to an inconvenient distance from the centre of the town, and university officers were empowered to enlist the co-operation of the railway staff in identifying members of the University on the station, and if any such members did not hold the degree of Master of Arts or Bachelor of Medicine or Civil Law, they could order the Company not to carry them for twenty-four hours, even if the fare had been paid. Any failure to comply with these regulations, or attempt at evasion (dropping passengers between stations was specified), made the Company liable to a £5 fine payable to Addenbrooke's Hospital or some designated charity.[198] Furthermore, no person was to be picked up or set down within three miles of Cambridge between 10 a.m. and 5 p.m. on a Sunday. This was to discourage Sunday excursions which, the Vice-Chancellor declared in 1851, were 'as distasteful to the University Authorities as they must be offensive to Almighty God, and to all right-minded Christians.'[199] When opened, the station was described by the *Railway Chronicle* as 'a long, flat and handsome brick building, with stone dressings, consisting of a double series of arcades . . . its architectural expression is rather Palladian.'[199] It had one long platform for use by both up and down trains and within a few months of the opening local interests were pressing for a more central station. The Company was prepared to accept, but the University objected to any measure that might disturb the academic calm of college life.[200]

Dissatisfaction with the siting of the station was a constant complaint, but it was not the only one. Both the public and the press became disenchanted with the Eastern Counties' performance by the end of 1845. They were first alarmed by a series of accidents, *The Cambridge Chronicle* stating, shortly after the opening of the line, that 'We have quite a glut of railway accidents just now; the market is overstocked. For two years one heard very little of these disasters; but now the papers are filled with matter-of-fact details.'[201] The *Independent Press* agreed and both advocated 'a large and effective system of inspection and control under the authority of responsible Government officers.'[202] The *Chronicle* also stated that it received 'complaints innumerable concerning the inconvenience and bad management at the Railway Station in this town . . . it is notorious that the

81

trains on the Eastern Counties line keep bad time . . . but irregularity is the grand fault.' [203] Accidents, delays, late arrival or non-arrival, made travelling on the Eastern Counties almost an adventure. The affairs of the Company appeared to everybody to be 'grossly mismanaged' and despite continued public criticism and complaints 'Delay, confusion, negligence is still the order of the day.' [204] Conditions such as these prompted Thackeray, some time later, to remark 'Even a journey on the Eastern Counties Railway comes to an end.' [205]

In an effort to improve matters the Company acquired the services of George Hudson, the 'Railway King', but as the *Chronicle* remarked a year later, 'new engines and new directors have as yet, we regret to say, produced but little improvement.' [206] The *Independent Press* urged Hudson to consider the need for a more central station and suggested Butts Green, far removed from the colleges, as a possible site. [207] The *Chronicle* advocated Midsummer Common or Mill Lane as alternatives but the University thwarted all proposals. [208] Hudson's efforts did not achieve the expected improvements and criticism of his methods became more bitter as the Company's financial position deteriorated. Large fare increases were the inevitable result and discontent was so widespread that the daily horse coach service to London was revived for eight months. [209] Hudson's association with the Company was terminated in 1849 and a new Board of Directors elected, but by now the reputation of the Company was at its lowest ebb. [210] The sluggishness of its trains and the embarrassed state of its finances were a byword.

Despite the development of this unpromising situation, the completion of the line from London to Cambridge in 1845 encouraged some optimism and many schemes were again proposed in a second attempt to make Cambridge a railway centre. While the *Advertiser* and *Independent Press* were excited at the prospect of so many new promotions, they wondered at the merit of 'rival company against rival company - competing scheme against competing scheme - old lines against new ones - trunk lines against branches.' [211] A public meeting was held in Cambridge Town Hall in 1845, convened by the Mayor, to consider the many new proposals. [212] A committee was appointed to investigate the merits of the various schemes and presented its report to a meeting in 1846.[213] It recommended the building of a new passenger station where Queen Anne Terrace once stood and favoured six schemes, among them the Cambridge to Oxford Railway.[214] Supported by the two Universities, the bill received the assent of Parliament in 1846, but the House of Lords only sanctioned the building of a line between Royston and Hitchin. This was later extended to Shepreth, a few miles south of Cambridge. The Great Northern Railway, which purchased the lease in 1850, was denied permission to build either the final stretch or a new station in Cambridge by the determined opposition of the Eastern Counties Railway and the University. The Oxford connection, through Bedford and Bletchley, was not completed until 1862. [215] By 1866, Cambridge had become a railway centre, with the trains of four separate companies using the one station. From the north came trains from Norwich, Huntingdon, Peterborough and Kettering, from the south trains arrived from London via Bishop's Stortford and Hitchin; from the east they came from Newmarket and Bury St. Edmunds, and west from Bedford and Oxford.[216]

Finally, what effect did the coming of the railways have on town and county? Agriculture was central to the region and had made but slow progress since the post 1815 slump in corn prices and, as a result, in the first fifty years of the nineteenth century, insecurity and hardship were widely prevalent in the county. The limited alternative sources of employment such as milling, malting, brewing and so on were equally dependent on agriculture and this situation was perpetuated by the inadequacy of the transport system. For the movement of freight much of the region depended on coastal shipping and the river traffic. Both were slow, unreliable, irregular and confirmed such ports as King's Lynn in comfortable commercial monopolies that were both costly and stagnant. Greater use of existing roads was not a solution because their condition was poor and their carrying capacity limited, with carriers' carts being unable to travel much more than twenty five miles a day. Offering cheap bulk transport at speed, the railways released the region from this type of restriction. The opening of the railway killed the river trade in Cambridge and promoted widespread unemployment among those who depended on it for their living.[217] However, it also added a new industry, a cement works, and a new quarter to the city.[218] By bringing the London market closer to Cambridge, it encouraged the development of brick and tile works at Cherry Hinton and Coldham's Lane, and lesser manufactures such as flour milling, brewing, malting and sausage making. Agriculture remained predominant, with Cambridgeshire now concentrating on the production of sugar beet, potatoes, fruit, flowers and livestock.

Although other factors were involved, it was no coincidence that the advent of railways was closely followed by the prosperous era of High Farming, when the loss of protection against foreign corn was countered by rationalisation and the widespread application of new techniques. Above all, therefore, the railway meant the advantages of closer ties with London, a wider choice of markets and readier availability at lower cost of coals, fertilisers, animal foods and other supplies, and these factors encouraged the cultivation of land hitherto regarded as marginal or inferior. Railways also stimulated internal migration and the drift from rural to urban areas. Travel at even the cheapest rates, and they were by no means cheap on Eastern Counties, remained a luxury for most, but the occasional visit to a town, or the even rarer excursion to London now became feasible. Cambridge people were slow to accept the many consequences brought by these changes, but they gradually came to adopt the more confident outlook that typified this 'age of improvement.'[219]

NOTES AND REFERENCES

1   *Camb. Chron.* 4 Feb., 15 April 1814; Cooper, *Annals* IV, pp. 506-7.
2   *Ibid.* 14 July 1814. See also *Narrative of the Celebration of Peace* (1814).

3   J.D. Chambers and G.E. Mingay, *The Agricultural Revolution* (1966), pp. 118-28. See also L.P. Adams, *Agricultural Depression and Farm Relief in England 1813-1852* (1932), Ch. 3.

4   *Camb. Chron.* and *Camb. Ind. Press,* 23 Feb., 1 Mar. 1816.

5   *Ibid.* 31 May, 1816.

6   *Ibid.* 21, 28 June, 5 July, 1816.

7   Hampson, *Poverty in Cambs.* p. 196. See also J.P.D. Dunbabin, *Rural discontent in nineteenth-century Britain* (1974), Ch. 3.

8   *Camb. Chron.* 8 Dec. 1826, 16 Feb. 1827.

9   *Ibid.* 27 July, 1832.

10   Contrasting interpretations can be found in R.J. White, *Waterloo to Peterloo* (1957), and Thompson, *Making of the English Working Class.*

11   Cradock, *Cambridge Union,* pp. 8-9.

12   *Camb. Chron.* 5 Jan. 1827, 7 Mar. 1823, 5 May 1820.

13   *Ibid.* 15 Feb. 1828. 29 Jan. 1830.

14   *Ibid.* 11 Mar., 8 May 1825.

15   *Ibid.* 9 Aug., 22 Nov. 1816, 23 July, 27 Aug. 1818, 20, 27 Aug. 1819.

16   *Ibid.* 9 Sept. 1831.

17   *Ibid.* 9 Sept. 1831.

18   *Huntingdon, Bedford, Peterborough and Cambridge Gazette* 1813-1819, (hereafter abbreviated to *H.B.P. and Camb. Gaz.*)

19   See Cooper, *Annals* IV, p. 523; Bowes, 'First Cambridge Newspapers', p. 357.

20   *The Northampton and Leamington Free Press,* 1831-34 (British Museum, Colindale).

21   *Camb. Ind. Press* 8 May 1819, 7 Jan. 1826, 18 Aug. 1832, 12 Jan. 1833, 1 June 1934. See also Timperley, *Dictionary of Printers,* p. 950. Bowes, *loc. cit.*, p. 357.

22   *H.B.P. and Camb. Gaz.* 12 Dec. 1818.

23   *Camb. Ind. Press* June, July, Aug. 1830.

24   *Ibid.* 12 Jan. 1833, 11 Aug. 1840.

25   *Ibid.* 7 Jan., 25 Mar. 1826.

26   *Ibid.* 26 Aug. 1837, 8 May 1819; Grant, *Newspaper Press,* III, p. 306.

27   *Ibid.* 7 Jan., 16 Dec. 1826, 8 Aug. 1840.

28   *Ibid.* 8, 15, 22 Aug. 1840.

29   *Ibid.* 8 Aug. 1840.

30   *H.B.P. and Camb. Gaz.* 28 Mar. 1818.

31   *Ibid.* 24 Feb. 1816, 28 Mar. 1818.

32   *Camb. Ind. Press* 22 Sept. 1832.

33   *H.B.P. and Camb. Gaz.* 5, 12 Oct. 1816, 11 Jan. 1817, 14 Nov. 1818.

34   *Camb. Ind. Press* 11 June 1831.

35   Read, *Press and People,* pp. 152-69.

36   *Camb. Ind. Press* 1 Oct. 1825, 27 May 1826; see also M. Scriblerus (pseud.), *The Ratland Feast* (1820), p. 11; *The Corporation Cambridge Chronicle* 22 Dec. 1829, June 1830.

37   *H.B.P. and Camb. Gaz.* 8 Feb. 1817; *Camb. Ind. Press* 29 Jan. 1831.

38   *Ibid.* 1 Mar. 1817.

39   *Camb. Ind. Press* 21 Aug. 1819.

40   *Ibid.* 26 June 1819.

41   *H.B.P. and Camb. Gaz.* 4 July 1818.

42 *Camb. Ind. Press* 2 April 1825, 6 Mar. 1819.
43 *Ibid.* 29 July 1826, 3 Mar. 1827.
44 *Ibid.* 28 Aug. 1827.
45 *Ibid.* 25 April 1825.
46 *Ibid.* 31 Dec. 1825.
47 *Ibid.* 18 Nov. 1826, 27 May 1820, 12 Dec. 1818.
48 *Ibid.* 3 Sept. 1825, 4 Mar. 1826, 17 Feb. 1827, 25 April 1829.
49 *Ibid.* 27 Oct. 1827, 10, 26 Jan. 1828.
50 *Ibid.* 8 Jan., 5 Feb. 1825.
51 *Ibid.* 5 Feb., 5, 28 Nov. 1825.
52 *Ibid.* 17 Nov. 1827.
53 *Ibid.*, 24 Jan. 1829; see also *The Boro'monger's Chronicle* July, Dec. 1831.
54 *Ibid.* 25 April 1829.
55 Read, *Press and People*, Ch. 4; A. Briggs, *Victorian Cities* (1963), p. 382.
56 Temple-Patterson, *Radical Leicester,* p. 28. Mitchell, *Newspaper Press,* p. 124.
57 W. Whittred, *A Letter to the Freemen of the Corporation of Cambridge* (1818).
58 *H.B.P. and Camb. Gaz.* 7, 14 Mar. 1818; *Camb. Chron.* 26 June 1818.
59 *Camb. Chron.* 26 June 1818.
60 Cooper, *Annals* IV, p. 522. *H.B.P. and Camb. Gaz.* Sept. 1818.
61 *Camb. Ind. Press* 13 Mar. 1819.
62 *Ibid.* 4, 11, 18 Dec. 1819; *Camb. Chron.* 3 Dec. 1819; See also J. Hodson, *The Cambridge Election* (1819).
63 *Camb. Ind. Press,* 22, 29 Jan., 23 Feb. 1820.
64 W. Hatfield, *The Trial and Acquittal of Mr. W. Hatfield on a false charge of riot and misdemeanor* (1820), p. 5.
65 *Camb. Chron.* 18 Feb. 1820, *Camb Ind. Press* 4, 11, March 1820.
66 *Camb. Ind. Press* 7 April, 1820.
67 *Ibid.* 14 April 1820.
68 *Ibid.* 26 Aug., 23 Sept. 1820; *Camb. Chron.* 9 Mar. 1821, 4 July 1823, 2 June 1828; Cooper, *Annals* IV, pp. 528-30, 542-4, 549.
69 *Camb. Ind. Press* 16, 23 Jan. 1832.
70 *Camb. Chron.* 22 June 1832.
71 *Camb. Ind. Press* 3 Nov. 1832.
72 *Camb. Chron.* and *Camb. Ind. Press* 14 Dec. 1832; see also D.C. Moore, *The Politics of Deference* (1976), pp. 45-46.
73 Gray, *Town of Cambridge,* p. 173. *Camb. Chron.* 16 Feb. 1827.
74 W. Hatfield, *A Full Report of the Important Toll Cause of Brett vs. Beales* (1826).
75 *Ibid.* pp. vii-viii.
76 *Camb. Chron.* 27 Jan. 1826; M.E. Keynes, *A House by the River: Newnham Grange to Darwin College* (1976), pp. 14-15.
77 *Camb. Chron.* 14 Dec. 1827.
78 *Camb. Ind. Press* 18 Jan. 1828, 18 July, 24 Oct. 1829.
79 *Camb. Chron.* and *Camb. Ind. Press* 18, 25 Dec. 1829. See also *The Cambridge Toll Cause* (1830).
80 *Camb. Ind. Press* 27 Feb., 6 Mar. 1830.
81 *Ibid.* 13 Mar. 1830.
82 *Ibid.* 19 April 1827, 5 June 1830; *Camb. Chron.* 25 Dec. 1829.

83   J.W. Croker, *Correspondence and Diaries* (ed.) L.J. Jennings, I, (1884), p. 321.
84   See Moore, *Politics of Deference*, Ch. 2.
85   See letter to *Camb. Ind. Press* 19 Feb. 1820.
86   *Camb. Chron.* and *Camb. Ind. Press* Mar. 1821, Feb. 1823, June 1826.
87   *Ibid.* 16 Mar. 1821.
88   *Ibid.* 21 Feb. 1823.
89   *Camb. Chron.* 10 Jan. 1823.
90   G.I.T. Machin, *The Catholic Question in English Politics 1820-30* (1964), p. 1.
91   *Camb. Ind. Press* 28 Nov. 1825.
92   *Camb. Chron.* 17 Dec. 1819.
93   *Ibid.* 16 May 1817, 20 April 1819, 16 Mar. 1821.
94   *Huntingdon, Bedford and Cambridge Journal* 26 Feb. 1825.
95   *Ibid.* 26 Feb. 1825.
96   *Ibid.* 26 Feb. 1825.
97   *Ibid.* 19 Mar., 30 April 1825, 3 June 1826, 24 Mar. 1827, 26 Jan. 1828.
98   *Ibid.* 5 Mar. 1825.
99   *Ibid.* 30 July 1825.
100 *Ibid.* 12 Mar., 14 May, 4 June 1825.
101 *Ibid.* 30 Dec. 1826, 2 April 1825, 4 Feb. 1826.
102 *Ibid.* 26 Feb. 1825, 29 Mar. 1828, 2 April 1825, 5 Aug. 1826, 3 Feb. 1827, 1 Oct. 1825.
103 *Ibid.* 9 July 1825.
104 *Camb. Chron.* 29 Nov. 1822.
105 *Ibid.* 4 Mar., 20 May, 30 Dec. 1825, 27 Jan. 1826.
106 *Camb. Ind. Press* 30 April, 7, 14 May 1825.
107 Machin, *The Catholic Question,* p. 69.
108 *Camb. Chron.* 16 June 1826.
109 *Camb. Ind. Press* 10 June 1826.
110 *The Times* 1 July 1826.
111 *Camb. Chron.* 23 June 1826.
112 *Camb. Chron.* May 1826.
113 *Ibid.* 2 June 1826.
114 Machin, *The Catholic Question,* p. 81.
115 *Camb. Chron.* 9 June 1826.
116 Quoted by Machin, *op. cit.* p. 82.
117 *Ibid.* p. 82.
118 Cradock, *Cambridge Union,* p. 21.
119 *Camb. Chron.* 6, 27 April 1827; F.G.A. Best, 'The Protestant Constitution and its Supporters' in *Transactions of the Royal Historical Society,* vol. 8, 1958.
120 *Camb. Ind. Press* 17 Mar. 1827.
121 *Ibid.* 5 July, 11 Oct. 1828.
122 *Camb. Chron.* 11 Oct. 1828.
123 *Ibid.* 13 Feb. 1829; Cooper, *Annals* IV, p. 559.
124 *Camb. Ind. Press* 14 Feb. 1829.
125 *Camb. Chron.* Mar. 1829; Cooper, *Annals* IV, p. 560.
126 *Ibid.* 3 April 1829.
127 *Ibid.* 29 Jan. , 23 July, 13, 20 Aug. 1830, 6, 13 May 1831.

128 *Camb. Ind. Press* 21 Mar. 1829.
129 D. Read, *The English Provinces c.1760-1960: a study in influence* (1964), pp. 80-81.
130 *Camb. Ind. Press* 7 May, 2 July, 13 Aug., 29 Oct. 1825.
131 *Camb. Chron.* 29 Jan. 1830.
132 *Camb. Ind. Press* 30 Jan. 1830.
133 *Camb. Chron.* 23 July 1830.
134 *Ibid.* 13 Aug. 1830.
135 *Camb. Ind. Press* 14 Aug. 1830; see also Mat Wildfire, (pseud), *Squibiana: a collection of addresses, songs, and other effusions published during the late election* (1831).
136 *Camb. Ind. Press* 20 Aug. 1830.
137 *Camb. Chron.* 20 Aug. 1830.
138 *Camb. Ind. Press* 14 Aug. 1830.
139 *Ibid.* 7 Jan. 1832; M. Brock, *The Great Reform Act* (1973), Ch. 4.
140 *Camb. Chron.* 24 June 1831.
141 *Camb. Ind. Press* 5 Mar. 1831.
142 *Camb. Chron.* 24 Feb. 1832.
143 *Ibid.* 2 Mar. 1832.
144 *Digested Report of the Evidence taken before the Corporation Commissioners* (1833) pp. 24-25; *Camb. Chron.* 8 Nov. 1833.
145 *Camb. Chron.* 4 Jan. 1833.
146 *Ibid.* 18 Mar. 1831.
147 *Ibid.* 14 May 1831; *Camb. Chron.* 13 May 1831.
148 *Camb. Chron.* 29 April 1831.
149 *Camb. Ind. Press* 7 May 1831.
150 *Camb. Chron.* 14 Oct. 1831, *Camb. Ind. Press* 22, 29 Oct. 1831.
151 *Camb. Chron.* 13 May, Aug., Sept., 1831.
152 *Ibid.* 9 Sept. 1831.
153 *Ibid.* 5 Aug., 15 July 1831.
154 *Ibid.* 3 June, 23 Dec. 1831.
155 *Ibid.* 10 June 1831, 6 Jan. 1832, 2 Dec. 1831.
156 *Ibid.* 22 July 1831.
157 *Ibid.* 7 Oct. 1831.
158 *Ibid.* 19 Aug. 1831.
159 *Camb. Ind. Press* 7, 28 Jan., 2 June 1832.
160 *Ibid.* 24 Jan. 1831, 22 Dec. 1832.
161 *Ibid.* 15, 22 Dec. 1832.
162 Moore, *Politics of Deference*, p. 54.
163 *Camb. Chron.* 30 May 1831, 31 Mar. 1851; Cooper, *Annals* IV, p. 517; V, p. 30.
164 *Ibid.* 6 Jan. 1833.
165 *Ibid.* 22 Sept. 1849.
166 *Camb. Ind. Press* 10, 17 Sept. 1842.
167 *The New Cambridge Guide* (1868), p. 172.
168 A.B. Gray, *Cambridge Revisited* (1921, reprinted 1974); *Camb. Chron.* 22 Sept. 1849.
169 *Camb. Chron.* 30 Jan. 1836, 24 June 1837.
170 *Ibid.* 9 Nov. 1844, Cooper, *Annals* IV, pp. 657, 706.
171 *Camb. Chron.* 3, 17 April 1847.

172 *Cambridge Advertiser and University Herald* (1846-50), 14 April, 19 May 1847.
173 *Victoria County History,* Cambs. II, (1848) pp. 341-51
174 *Camb. Chron.* 12 Mar. 1808. For information on town charity schools see: *Report on the Charities of Cambridgeshire* VI, (1839).
175 L. Stone, 'Literacy and Education in England 1640-1900' in *Past and Present* no. 42, (Feb.) 1969.
176 See G.F.A. Best, 'The Religious Difficulties of National Education in England 1800-1870' in *Cambridge Historical Journal* XII, (1956).
177 *Camb. Chron.* 1, 29 June, 23 Nov., 7 Dec. 1839.
178 *Cambridge Advertiser and Free Press* 5 Aug. 1840.
179 See C.H. Cooper, *Memorials of Cambridge* III, (1860-66), pp. 163-4.
180 Hobsbawm and Rudé, *Captain Swing,* p. 16.
181 A.J. Peacock, 'Village radicalism in East Anglia 1800-1850' in Dunbabin, *Rural discontent.*
182 *Report of the Select Committee on Agricultural Distress* (1836), VIII, pt. 1, 115 ff.
183 J. Caird, *English Agriculture in 1850-51* (1852), pp. 467-8.
184 *Cambridge Advertiser and Free Press* 15 Oct. 1845.
185 D.I. Gordon, *A Regional History of the Railways of Great Britain,* V, (1968), p. 135.
186 R.B. Fellows, *Railways to Cambridge, actual and proposed,* (1948, reprinted 1976), p. 1.
187 Cooper, *Annals* IV, p. 601.
188 Fellows, *Railways to Cambridge,* pp. 7-8.
189 *Camb. Chron.* 3 Oct. 1834; *Camb. Ind. Press* 4 Oct. 1834.
190 *Ibid.* 31 Oct., 7, 14 Nov. 1834.
191 *Camb. Ind. Press* 16 Aug. 1845.
192 *Camb. Chron.* 6 April 1844.
193 *Cambridge Advertiser and Free Press* 16 Sept. 1840, 8 July 1840.
194 *Camb. Chron.* 8 Feb. 1843.
195 *Ibid.* 6 April, 12 Oct. 1844.
196 *Ibid.* 29 Mar. 1845.
197 *Ibid.* 25 July, 2 Aug. 1845.
198 *Camb. Ind. Press* 20 April 1844; Fellows, *Railways to Cambridge,* p. 11.
199 Quoted by Gray, *Town of Cambridge,* p. 185.
200 *Cambridge Advertiser and Free Press* 30 July 1845.
201 *Camb. Chron.* 23 Aug. 1845.
202 *Ibid.* and *Camb. Ind. Press* 9, 23 Aug. 1845.
203 *Camb. Chron.* 23 Aug. 1845.
204 *Ibid.* 6 Sept., 30 Aug., 20 Sept. 1845.
205 Quoted by C.J. Allen, *The Great Eastern Railway* (1955), p. 163.
206 *Camb. Chron.* 22 Nov. 1845.
207 *Camb. Ind. Press* 22 Nov. 1845.
208 *Ibid.* 22 Nov. 1845; Fellows, *Railways to Cambridge,* p. 17.
209 *Ibid.* 28 Aug. 1847.
210 Allen, *Great Eastern,* pp. 18-19.
211 *Cambridge Advertiser and Free Press* 15 April 1846.
212 *Camb. Chron.* 22 Nov. 1845.
213 *Ibid.* 24 Jan. 1846.

214   *Ibid.* 24 Jan. 1846.
215   Fellows, *op. cit.* pp. 20-23.
216   *Ibid.* p. 21.
217   Reeve, *Cambridge,* p. 99.
218   *Victoria County History Cambs.* III (1959), p. 98.
219   *Camb. Chron.* 16 Jan. 1847.

4

The Impact of Reform
1832-1850

I

During this final period there were no changes in the policies advocated by the editors of the rival newspapers in the town. Both newspapers experimented by enlarging or contracting the size of their publications, and both endeavoured further to please their patrons by improving their type and layout.[1] The *Chronicle* began to .issue a supplement when 'the press of advertisements' was particularly heavy, and brought itself into line with the *Independent Press* in 1837 by changing its date of publication from Friday to Saturday. [2] The numbers of advertisements in both papers, approximately one hundred per week, and the incoming revenue, about fifty pounds per week from all sources in the 1830s and seventy five pounds per week in the 1840s, also remained fairly equal.[3] As already noted, editorials were first introduced into the *Chronicle* during the debate on the Reform Bill. Charles Edward Brown, the young partner of Francis Hodson, was a Tory editor of sterner quality, and transformed the paper into a much more lively defender of Conservatism in the 1830s and 1840s. He was made coroner for the town in 1834 and in 1837 became sole proprietor of the *Chronicle* when the partnership with Hodson was 'mutually dissolved.' [4] In 1846 and 1868 he was elected Mayor of Cambridge and on each occasion remained in office for one year. [5] Although the *Chronicle* maintained its former position, it failed to increase its circulation during these decades and continued to sell about 1800 copies per week. University and borough council support ensured that advertising revenue did not fall [6] and therefore he was opposed to the movement which pressed for a reduction in the newspaper stamp duty, being convinced that the real object of such radical demands was 'the promotion of universal suffrage, by means of a cheap, free and unshackled press.' [7] Brown remained in control of the *Chronicle* until 1849, when he sold out to one of his printers, C.W. Naylor. [8]

During the same period Weston and James Hatfield increased the circulation of the *Independent Press* by one third. Shortly after its move to Cambridge in 1819 the *Independent Press* was probably achieving a circulation equal to that of the *Chronicle* and it retained its position until the reduction of the stamp duty in 1836. [9] By 1841 its circulation had increased to 2230 weekly, and under its new proprietor, Henry Smith, it reached 2600 by 1845, now selling almost 800 copies more than the *Chronicle* per week. [10] As a middle-class, reforming editor, Hatfield had welcomed the reduction in the 'taxes on knowledge' which had lowered the price of the *Independent Press,* and the *Chronicle,* from 7d to 4½d. The reduction, he stated, 'seems to have stricken our Tory contemporaries with horror', but he maintained that the taxes were 'a clog upon knowledge and an impediment to the free discussion of those matters which involve the general interests of society . . . clearly shown by the number of unstamped papers . . . which meet with an extensive and a ready sale.' [11] Hatfield believed that newspapers were essentially national in character, and feared the localism that might occur if the Post Office withdrew the free postage policy that existed. [12] For the same reason he continued to publish full parliamentary reports at the expense of local gossip and intelligence because 'we confess that we have to aim at something higher.' [13] Informed public opinion was necessary if changes in the political scene were to be fully understood. During the debate on the Reform Bill and the Corn Laws he stressed that he spoke in the national interest. However he accepted that 'we incur the risk of giving offence to a considerable body of our subscribers . . . but as the duties of a journalist are not of a particular character, we must be content to incur partial censure, in order to effect a public good.'[14] Hatfield died in 1837 aged forty three. He had been editor of the *Independent Press* for twenty years. His obituary stated that having become 'the political representative of the Reformers of his native and adjoining counties [he] courageously fought their battles - thro' evil and thro' good report - with a view to the attainment of all possible good, calculated to benefit and enlighten his fellow-man, and enfranchise his brother citizens.' [15] He had successfully carried on the liberal tradition of Benjamin Flower, and through his efforts major reform issues were kept alive in town, county and University. Cambridge opinion would have been far less interesting without his contribution.

The newspaper was moved to new premises in Market Hill in January 1840, and almost exactly one year later the Hatfield connection with the *Independent Press* was broken when it was taken over by Henry Smith. He did, however, maintain the liberal tradition of the paper for the rest of the 1840s. It also successfully resisted the attempt to establish two rival liberal newspapers in the town during these years. The first was *The Cambridge Guardian,*[16] printed and published by Samuel Wilson, in 1838. Only two copies of this newspaper have survived and politically they are both liberal in tone. They expressed the hope that 'Dissenters will approve *The Cambridge Guardian.'* Nevertheless, the newspaper was to prove no real competitor to the *Independent Press.* Of much more importance was *The Cambridge General Advertiser,* the first number of which appeared in January 1839. It began as a simple advertising sheet printed by William Metcalfe and Jonathan Palmer at their offices in Green Street. The first editorial claimed that its aim was strictly commercial, but it also intended to publish some matters of public importance, 'carefully collected from the leading Journals.' [17] It displayed approximately twenty-five advertisements and was offered 'gratis.' By July it was established as a new Cambridge newspaper entitled *The Cambridge Advertiser and Free Press,* published on Wednesday and costing fourpence. [18] The new editor was William Atkinson Warwick. It was a direct rival to the *Independent Press* because, although they differed slightly on certain issues, the political, social and economic attitudes of the two newspapers had much in common. It rejected the suggestion that the establishment of a second liberal paper in the county would be 'injurious to the Liberal Cause', and insisted that this was merely a fiction disseminated by certain 'Interested Parties.' [19] In an effort to stress the difference between them, it continued to publish mid-week, maintained its lower price and paid a certain amount of attention to the printing of lithographs. [19] By 1846 it was publishing about fifty advertisements per week and selling about seven hundred copies in the town and surrounding counties. [20] In a bid to increase its circulation among members of the University it changed its title to *The Cambridge Advertiser and University Herald* in 1846, but appears to have made little impact in the traditional territory of the *Chronicle*. The new editor, W.J. Cannon, was later forced to raise the price of the *Advertiser* to fivepence. [21]

From its foundation it favoured 'the principle of Constitutional Reform', being critical of abuses in Church and State and advocating popular rights and free institutions. [22] It also urged 'the amelioration of the condition of the lower classes of society - the just and equitable government of Ireland - and the vote by Ballot.' [23] It opposed the harshness of the new Poor Law and the centralising powers of the Commissioners, which it regarded as 'much too extensive and far too undefined.' [24] Towards Ireland it wished to see the government initiate a policy of justice and liberality because coercion had always failed. The miseries of Ireland, it maintained, were as manifold as her crimes, and it suggested legislation giving 'some security for the Irish peasant against wholesale eviction.' [25] The rights of humanity as well as the rights of property, it argued, were deserving of respect. The corruption of local politics made it favour the ballot 'for without the Ballot, freedom of election is an unsubstantial shadow and independence of action but a name, and nothing more.' [26] The two major policies it advocated during the 1840s were state intervention in education and repeal of the Corn Laws. It commented that it was 'a lamentable fact, that in this large town, containing probably 25,000 inhabitants, there are not more than about 1200 children of the poor classes . . . who are receiving daily instruction.' [27] It therefore gave full support to the admittedly limited Whig education proposals of 1839, 'a subject upon which ministers are considerably in advance of the public mind', and condemned Wesleyans and Anglicans for their opposition. [28] In the same spirit it recommended the abolition of the Corn Laws and rejected the argument that farmers should be privileged, or that they were 'more highly taxed than the rest of the Queen's subjects.' [29] Instead of depending on the Corn Laws it urged farmers to improve, rationalise and economise, and hoped the Agricultural Societies would advocate a similar policy 'instead of denunciations of the League, attacks on Sir Robert Peel, or whining complaints about the lowness of prices and the gloominess of farmers' prospects.' [30] Despite its efforts, the initiative in the battle of opinion in Cambridge remained with the *Chronicle* and the *Independent Press*, and by 1850 the succession of editors, plus promises of better service and attention to readers' wishes, clearly showed that the attempt to establish a successful new paper in the town had failed. [31] The last number was published in December of that year.

II

The passing of the Reform Bill was greeted with great enthusiasm throughout the county. Celebration dinners and festivities were held in almost every town and village. Cambridge Whigs probably overrated their victory as much as the Tories exaggerated their defeat. Nevertheless, the majority of the Whigs in government realised that, despite difficulties within the party, if useful and progressive reforms did not follow, their reform laurels might go to make a radical bonfire. [32] The policy of reform by instalments was adopted, but while these measures were being pushed through Parliament the degree of Whig support, both inside and outside the House of Commons, declined. The House of Lords did not help with its frequent amendments and occasional rejections of important Whig measures. As a result of these political tactics the more radical Whigs began to demand a reform of this predominantly Tory institution. Reformers such as Hatfield, however, stressed the difficulties involved, and warned against adopting any measures that might split the party. [33] Throughout the county people waited eagerly to see what benefits the Reform Act would bring. In fact, both the pessimistic predictions of the Tories, and hopeful expectations of the Radicals, turned out to be unfounded.

The *Chronicle* proved a stubborn critic of most of the Whig measures passed in the years following 1832, except those, such as factory reform, which proved an embarrassment to the Whigs. It even opposed the terms of the bill for the abolition of slavery, favouring, as did C.P. Yorke at the 1832 election, a gradual approach. [34] Weston Hatfield accused the editor of the *Chronicle* of suppressing that part of Yorke's speech at Wisbech where he stated that the emancipation of slaves was 'a violation of the right of property', sentiments Hatfield regarded as 'repugnant to every Christian feeling.' [35] Meanwhile Samuel Wells continued to insist that English 'white slaves' in factories in the North had prior claims to the sympathy of the people of Britain. [36] When the measure was finally passed, the *Chronicle* felt that a unilateral approach carried out with such rapidity was neither just nor sensible. Whilst not being entirely satisfied by the measure, Hatfield accepted the bill as an act of justice; 'We shall be told of the rights of property, and of the interests of the planter, but what are these when weighed against the rights of man?'[37]

After the disclosures of Sadler's Report on infant labour in the factories, the *Chronicle* was convinced that 'there was more actual suffering, more brutalizing, heartless tyranny - more waste of life' in the industrial North, than in the West Indian plantations and expressed horror at the conditions of labour and the avarice of manufacturers. [38] It therefore welcomed unreservedly Althorp's Act of 1833, which limited hours of work for children in the factories. [39] As the factory question recurred throughout the next ten years, the *Chronicle* maintained a consistent attitude. Professor Pryme was condemned for not giving more support to factory reform, and John Bright for having the temerity to call Graham's proposal in 1843 a measure of 'tinkering legislative interference' while he became rich from the toil of 'the white slaves of Rochdale.' [40] It also supported Ashley's Ten Hours Bill, finally passed in 1847, and reproached Peel's government for its caution and timidity in not accepting the measure earlier. [41] Hatfield, like Pryme, was not opposed to all factory legislation, but believed that the shortening of the working day was not in the interests of the working-class. His approach was similar to that of Edward Baines of *The Leeds Mercury*, and he printed extracts from the latter's newspaper in support of this theory. [42] In 1838 Pryme opposed the further reduction of hours, fearing a situation in which 'the age from nine to thirteen is condemned to utter unproductiveness.' [43] For similar reasons the *Independent Press* was against the Ten Hours Bill brought forward in 1846. Its attitude was dictated by the laws of political economy:' *'laissez faire'* must rule. With respect to *The Times* and the many philanthropists who supported the measure, the editor felt that 'their attempt to interfere with the laws of the labour market, and the rights of demand and supply, is a delusion . . . The less we interfere the better . . . in the fair pursuits of trade and manufactures the 'leave us alone' principle is ever found in the long run to be the best.' [44] In his summary of the achievements of the first Whig ministry, Hatfield did not include the 1833 Factory Act.[45] *The Cambridge Advertiser* welcomed factory reform. While at one with the *Independent Press* on the principle of non-interference in trade, it maintained that interference was acceptable in matters of social policy and when humanity, religion or morality was involved, political economy should give way. [46]

Linked with the factory movement of the 1830s was the agitation concerning the Poor Law. The problem had always been a serious one in Cambridge, but many were not sure about the wisdom of the Whig measure of reform in 1834. Briefly, the act divided England into 64 Poor Law Unions each with its own workhouse. Outdoor relief was abolished and the alternative to work was the strict regime of the workhouse where conditions were to be 'less eligible' than those of the poorest industrious labourer. The Poor Law was to be a powerful inducement to self-help and consequently was more concerned with pauperism than poverty. [47] While Malthusians welcomed it wholeheartedly, believing that the allowance system removed the fear of hunger that kept men industrious, the editors of the *Chronicle* and the more liberal *Advertiser* were not so sure that such a centralised system could operate successfully.[48] They viewed Poor Law (and factory) reform with the same Tory paternalistic spirit and condemned the harshness of its provisions, seeing it as a typical product of the new political economy. They insisted that the needs of agricultural and industrial areas were different, that the powers of the newly constituted local boards were 'oppressively exercised',[49] and that conditions in the workhouses were generally inhuman because there was so little flexibility in the system, only 'one house, one dietary, one set of rules for all. The strong and the weak, the young and the aged, the idle and the unfortunate.' [50] They disliked the fact that the workhouse was the keystone of the system, and also the stringency of administrative provisions that decreed no relief outside the workhouse itself. [51]

The Rev. F.H. Maberly voiced the local opposition to the new scheme on behalf of the poor and many of the county doctors, clergy and gentry. [52] He called town meetings and expressed his views to thousands of people, notably at

Illustrations of the 'Whig' Poor Laws

Cambridge, Royston, Huntingdon and Ely, from 1834 to 1836.[53] He denied
that pauperism was wilful and praised the old system as being at least humane.
The new law, however, was 'tyrannical, unconstitutional, antiscriptural,
antichristian, illegal, unnatural cruel and impolitic in the extreme' and bedevilled
by reasoning that demanded 'a man was to work whether he could get it or
not.'[54] He condemned the breaking up of families, the ruthless administration,
the inadequate workhouse diet and lack of provision of any effective medical
service.[55] The actual cases of hardship quoted by correspondents to the
Chronicle provide convincing testimony to the truth of the facts.[56] County
agricultural labourers were Maberly's main audience, and he hoped by use of
the mass meeting and petition to get the act suspended. The county agricultural
labourers respected him for his stand against the government on the issue. He
informed them that he was under threat of suspension because of his efforts on
their behalf and had been warned by the Home Secretary that he would be held
responsible for any riotous disturbances that occurred at his meetings.[57] At
Royston in 1836 labourers confidently expected that they were being assembled
to pull down the workhouse![58] When he was arrested by the new Cambridge
town police in 1837 for trying to speak about the Poor Law at the borough
election nomination, the people 'rescued' him from the town gaol and bore him
back to Parker's Piece on their shoulders, where he addressed them for another
hour on the subject.[59]

There was a decided difference of opinion about the wisdom of the Poor Law
Amendment Act between Hatfield on the one hand and the Rev. Maberly and

the editors of the *Chronicle* on the other. Characteristically, Hatfield accepted the teachings of Malthus and therefore welcomed the bill enthusiastically, agreeing with one of his correspondents that the measure, though not perfect, was in advance of 'the spirit of the times.'[60] He condemned Maberly's campaign to discredit the bill, and often devoted editorials to the task of informing public opinion about the various misconceptions the 'Reverend gentleman' was propagating. [61] Hatfield denied that relief was only available in the workhouse, or that the act was at all 'harsh or oppressive towards the virtuous poor.' [62] He maintained that the Rev. Maberly had been 'led away by feelings of philanthropy which do him credit, but at the same time, we are sure that he has much to answer for, in having increased the prejudices and strengthened the erroneous opinions of the poor concerning the enactments and probable consequences of the law.' [63] He suggested that Maberly and his 'reverend accomplices' Clack and Lund return to their parishes, and quietly remain among their own flocks, where they would certainly find a refutation of their arguments.[64] He also stressed that the act was carried 'by the united efforts of Whigs and Tories', and so had little sympathy with opponents of the measure, 'whose hearts are larger than their heads; who fancy that the state has to do everything for the poor, and the poor nothing for themselves.' [65] The *Chronicle*, Hatfield insisted, by supporting the demagoguery of Maberly was merely indulging in factious opposition. Prior to the election of 1837 Hatfield proclaimed that this was the major reform of the Whig party, and urged the electors not to be misled by Tory propaganda or protestations that they were the real friends of the poor, because Tory sympathy, as given to the people of Manchester in 1819, merely amounted to 'the sabre and the hoof.' [66] Despite its criticisms, the *Chronicle* was prepared to admit that the new Poor Law had its merits, one of the most important being the 'apparent saving of money to the ratepayers.' [67] However, if the system was to be made permanent, the editor of the *Chronicle* believed that feelings of humanity made certain amendments necessary. Hatfield had no such reservations, being convinced that it was 'one of the most beneficial laws that human wisdom ever devised.'[68]

In 1835 the Municipal Corporations Act was passed, and reformers in the town welcomed it as a logical corollary to the Reform Act. Demands for this reform had figured prominently among the objectives of local radicals prior to 1832, many of whom regarded these oligarchic bodies as more corrupt and cramping than the unreformed House of Commons. The Act terminated the Rutland ascendancy in Cambridge. The *Chronicle* had made its position clear as early as 1833, when the first Corporation Commissioners visited Cambridge. [69] Brown and Hodson insisted that the powers vested in the Corporation Commissioners were illegal. This was hardly surprising, as Brown's family was one of those named as having derived considerable advantages from Rutland's connection with the corporate body. [70] The results of the enquiry into the activities of the Cambridge Corporation were reported in detail in the *Independent Press,* [71] and trenchantly summed up in a leading article of *The Times* in 1833, which stated: 'Probably no judicial investigation into a public trust ever brought to life more shameless profligacy or more inveterate dishonesty, more barefaced venality in politics, a more heartless disregard of the claims of the poor in the provision of funds left for their benefit, or a more degrading subservience to the views of the rich when they appeared in the shape of patrons or distributors of places; a more insatiable cupidity in the corporate officers to enrich themselves with the corporate property, or a more entire neglect of their duties and function as magistrates, than are presented by the evidence now before us.' [72] The Corporation struggled against its fate, but was eventually dissolved in 1835 and a new town council elected in its place.

The *Chronicle* condemned the act principally 'because the seeds of democracy are scattered through it', but accepted it after the Lords' amendments in September 1835 which divided towns into wards, raised the property voting qualifications and kept Dissenters from interfering with Corporation Church property. [73] It still disliked the ratepayer franchise instituted by the act, for it knew that under such a system control of the Corporation would pass to the Whigs and their supporters, the merchants, shopkeepers and Dissenters in the town. The first elections in December confirmed this fear and resulted in a sweeping majority for the reforming party. According to the *Chronicle,* the changes which followed the operation of the act were political partisanship of the worst kind, old corporate members being 'turned out by a kind of lynch law, Town Clerks and Coroners, for the sin of Conservatism.'[74] In its opinion the new men who replaced them were inferior, less educated, and therefore less respected, and simply not capable of 'a more judicious administration of Borough property.' [75] Most of its reports on the work of the new town council throughout 1836 and 1837 condemn this Whig exclusiveness and lack of administrative experience. However, the *Independent Press* had only praise for the measure and the new Council: 'there are no secret Council meetings now, no guzzling, no corruption. Everything is carried on with a due regard to prudence, economy, honesty and public decency, and the public is admitted, to give them an opportunity of scrutinizing the conduct of those whom they have placed in office.' [76]

In many respects it was the *Chronicle* that proved correct - the age of civic pride had not yet arrived. The functions of the new councils were few, and cheap government was regarded as more desirable than efficient government. Lack of funds and administrative drive stifled any initiative that existed, and most of the limited work of town improvement in Cambridge was still left to the unambitious Improvement Commissioners.

III

Another problem in the 1830s was neither social nor economic, but religious. The reforming zeal of the Whigs, and their alliance with the Dissenters, made many staunch supporters of the Church of England fear that the new Parliament would reform not only the State but also the Church. The *Independent Press* maintained that this approach was acceptable: 'Not merely the wants of the people demand this reform; but the interests of the Church, in its spiritual sense, require it also.'[77] Radicals were calling for an unqualified disestablishment of the

Church, and a complete separation of Church and State and some, like Cobbett, also demanded property confiscation, as well as a cessation of the Church's connection with the Universities and its control over education. Extreme Tory fears, however, proved unjustified, and radical hopes of a severance of the connection between Church and State were dashed long before 1837. It appeared by that date that the Whigs, like the Tories, were not over-eager to remedy all the grievances of Dissenters.[78] The *Chronicle* had always displayed an especial interest in the affairs of the established Church, and because of its support for the University, in Anglican education as well. It had supported all three prior to 1832 and continued to do so in the 1830s. It expected the new Parliament to turn its attention to Church reform but made it clear that it would 'oppose all schemes of spoliation, and protect vested rights.'[79] However, it paid little attention to the writings, or activities, of members of the Oxford Movement.[80] Hatfield was a confirmed 'supporter of the Dissenters' and therefore advocated Church reform, especially the commutation of tithes both in England and Ireland. However, he disagreed with Dissenters who petitioned for the separation of Church and State, and urged them to campaign merely for their civil rights, and equality with Anglicans.[81] Inevitably concessions had to be made, yet the Church not only survived the attack but managed to revive. She manifested her new vitality by reforming herself, and by so doing she grew stronger. By 1837 the *Chronicle* was able to refer with satisfaction to 'the general burst of feeling throughout the country in favour of ancient Protestant privileges.'[82]

The University was still practically the preserve of the Church of England - very few undergraduates were not at least nominal Anglicans. The *Chronicle* was adamant that 'the connection between them should be indissoluble.'[83] The Whigs in the Senate were still in a minority, but they continued to campaign for the abolition of religious tests. The attack was led in 1833 by the Dissenter R.M. Beverley, with his famous *Letter to his Royal Highness the Duke of Gloucester, Chancellor, on the present corrupt state of the University of Cambridge.* It was an exaggerated and lurid attempt to discredit Anglican undergraduates. Professor Sedgwick demonstrated this pamphlet to be both ill-informed and malicious, and defended the University in *The Times* and *Leeds Mercury*.[84] The assault failed and even Hatfield agreed that the pamphlet was given to absurd exaggerations. The reform group then turned its attention to University influence in borough politics. Hatfield was convinced by Professor Henslow's pamphlet that the University was given to 'direct and extensive interference . . . not always unaccompanied by threats or promises', and supported his successful campaign against bribery in the years following.[85] In later years the *Cambridge Advertiser* also denounced University interference and frequently condemned it in editorials.[86] Hatfield also welcomed the founding of the non-sectarian University of London and campaigned for a national, secular system of education. He was disappointed when the Whigs were forced to withdraw their scheme for a national system in 1839.[87] The *Advertiser* agreed that 'Education we must have, and that from the state . . . individuals cannot do it: the state therefore is the only resource.'[88] The editor of the *Chronicle* dissented, proclaiming that 'rather than see these mischievous principles carried out in our native town, we should prefer no education at all.'[89] It joined in the Anglican uproar against the 'infidel scheme' proposed in 1839 but supported the Tory proposal put forward in 1843 which was highly favourable to the established Church.[90]

The *Chronicle* displayed unusual interest in Ireland in this period, partly because the Whigs were so preoccupied with O'Connell and Irish problems, but also because 'for many years almost every Irish question has been treated in some respects as a Church question.'[91] Its policy towards O'Connell and Irish Catholics remained extremely hostile. Every major editorial on O'Connell, 'the noble pensioner of the poor', condemned his attempts to repeal the Union and subvert the established Church in Ireland, as well as his personal power-seeking, greed, and tyranny over the Catholic majority.[92] The *Chronicle's* solution to the Irish question was a mixture of coercion and conciliation - an Irish Poor Law and tougher government action to curb agitation and law-breaking. It maintained that Ireland had been treated too well in the past, 'very like a great overgrown boy, who has been petted and spoiled . . . We fear Pat must be regularly put to school, and have a good deal of training, before he will be a good boy, and grow up into a useful member of society.'[93] The *Independent Press* and the *Advertiser* continued the policy of Benjamin Flower, and were much more liberal in their attitude to Ireland. The task of the *Independent Press* in this instance was the important one of educating public opinion: 'We must really begin to remodel our opinions respecting Ireland. We must learn to judge of her on the broad and liberal principles of eternal justice; and not according to the dictates of a narrow-minded and selfish expediency.'[94] Hatfield refused to condemn O'Connell, or the Irish since they merely demanded justice for a people 'reduced by centuries of bad government to the lowest state of poverty and degradation.'[95] In his opinion England was the real culprit, 'the Cause of Irish Barbarism.'[96] Though he supported Whig policy in Ireland he was firmly against repeal of the Union. However, unlike the *Chronicle* he defended O'Connell's right to agitate peacefully for this cause. Peel (1841-46) over-came O'Connell's threat but it is significant that, following the latter's release from prison in 1844, a large parade of radicals and Irish, estimated at over two thousand, noisily celebrated in the streets of Cambridge.[97]

IV

Many Whigs expected that the Reform Bill would bring bribery and corruption in the borough to an end, but although the power of the Duke of Rutland had been extinguished and the number of voters in the town increased from two hundred to twelve hundred and fifty, corruption continued to exist. James Hatfield stated in 1838 that 'Intimidation, bribery and corruption are almost in as ripe and full luxuriance as they were before the passing of that which was promised to be an all healing measure.'[98] The fact was that the Cambridge voter had become accustomed to being bribed, and the system continued because it was so widespread. Both parties accepted that bribery was important in the boroughs.[99] In Cambridge by this time the parties were about equally divided and each accused the other of bribery in all the elections after 1832, though usually very little evidence was offered.[100] These were difficult years for the Tories in Cambridge. The Whigs, Pryme and Spring-Rice, were successful in 1832, and in the three elections that followed in the thirties. [101] On each occasion the *Chronicle* either accused the Whigs of bribery and intimidation or the Conservative voters of defection. In 1835 Pryme maintained that 'undue influence had been used against him and several acts of bribery committed'.[102] As a result of election events, Professor Henslow published his *Address to the Reformers of Cambridge*, which Hatfield printed in the *Independent Press*.[103] Henslow followed this activity in the cause of reform by bringing successful bribery actions against Mr. Canham and Mr. Fawcett. He was rewarded for his labours by a presentation from the Cambridge reformers and a slogan daubed on the walls of Corpus, 'Henslow, common informer.'[104] In 1836 F. Gunning and E. Foster, both of the 'Independent Party', brought a further action over bribery which does not appear to have been pursued.[105] In 1839, after Spring-Rice had been raised to the peerage, as Lord Monteagle, the *Chronicle* warned Conservative electors not to be 'over-zealous', and when Manners Sutton won the election, the Whig candidate, Mr. Gibson, accused the Conservatives of using 'gross corruption and fierce intimidation' to gain the seat.[106] The *Chronicle* stated that the Whigs were merely trying 'to veil their disappointment under the humbug of bribery.'[107] Hatfield had already accused the newly-founded Conservative Association of being instituted merely 'to accomplish the perfect servility of as large a number of voters as possible by the brutalising system of treating', and the indirect offer, or withdrawal of trade, as a bribe or threat.[108] Hatfield printed four editions on the Saturday that the bribery scandal was exposed - described in more direct language by the *Advertiser* as 'low, grovelling, base, dirty BRIBERY.'[109] A meeting of Whigs and reformers petitioned the House of Commons, naming one Samuel Long as the chief agent of Tory bribery.[110] The Committee resolved, after hearing the evidence, that Manners Sutton was guilty, by his agents, of bribery, and deprived him of his seat.[111]

It appeared from the evidence that an extensive and corrupt system of treating prevailed at the election. Apart from direct bribery one hundred and fifty pounds was paid 'to messengers, flag bearers and persons employed to walk before the band.'[112] These payments plus extravagant wages often amounted to half the total cost of the election. The *Chronicle* rejected such evidence maintaining rather lamely that election time was a time for gaiety and frivolity, and justifiable expenses, not a time 'to investigate the doling out of every bit of bread and cheese, or every half pint of beer!'[113] It appeared from later evidence that Samuel Long was merely the most notorious agent of bribery. In 1839 he received a fifty pound fee for his services to the Conservative party. His method was to inspect the rate books and find out who was in arrears, and once bribed, a voter was bribeable ever after. Long distributed approximately £400 in the elections of 1839 and 1841, £600 in 1843 and over £1000 in 1845 much of which was spent in last-minute bribes, on behalf of the Conservative member

Mr. Kelly, at the Star and Garter public house.[114] The Bribery Act was obviously a dead letter and to solve the problem the Radicals and Hatfield recommended the secret ballot, a further extension of the suffrage and shorter parliaments.[115] Hatfield had supported the introduction of the ballot since 1832, but had been reluctant at first 'to thrust the question upon the immediate attention of Parliament', being fully aware of the fact that 'the Whig party are not unanimous upon this point.'[116] For most of the thirties the two Whig representatives of the borough were actually on opposing sides, Pryme being in favour of the measure, and Spring-Rice against.[117] By 1837 Hatfield and his associates regarded themselves 'as firm, strenuous and uncompromising advocates of Vote by Ballot',[118] and considered the time had now come to make it an open question. Hatfield devoted eight major editorials to the subject in that year and urged the townspeople to petition in its favour.[119]

From the outset the *Chronicle* rejected the open ballot with equal determination, maintaining that the country would 'gain but little by changing the manly, straightforward plan of openly supporting a candidate, for the shuffling, prevaricating, hypocritical system of giving a blind vote for one, with the name of the other on the lips. The balloting box would be a very un-English substitute for the open poll.'[120] Though the ballot issue had become an open question in the Whig party by 1840, the government showed little interest in introducing a bill for its adoption into the House of Commons.

Much of the subsequent radical and working-class frustration was channelled into Chartism in the 1840s. It was never a powerful movement in the agricultural areas of England, but the *Chronicle* still demanded strong action from the government, and asked if it was wise for the executive to act weakly 'while Chartism is so powerfully raising its maddened head and gory hand.'[121] James Hatfield, the new editor of the *Independent Press,* and the newly established *Cambridge Advertiser* were equally opposed to the movement, and also urged the government to take strong and decisive measures against the leaders of 'this bloodthirsty and most brutal agitation.'[122] For once the *Independent Press* found itself in agreement with the *Chronicle.* Even more surprisingly, this was so when the *Chronicle* condemned the alliance of Tories and Chartists in the Nottingham election of 1841.[123] To Hatfield the movement illustrated two important points. The first was the need for education: the Chartist rising at Newport was in his opinion 'a stronger argument in favour of National Education on a broad and rational basis, than a hundred speeches in and out of Parliament.' Secondly, the movement had exploded the myth of 'the finality of the Reform Bill.'[124]

An attempt to hold a Chartist meeting in Cambridge during the period failed. It was reported that a man had been busy on Market Hill for several days collecting signatures for the Charter, and later it was announced that a meeting would be held by Mr. P. M'Grath, financial secretary of the Chartist Land Company and a prominent debater for the movement.[125] According to the *Chronicle* it created some excitement in the town, 'as few of them had seen a real living and speaking Chartist.'[126] The town magistrates, however, were not prepared to take any chances and banned the meeting. Perhaps it was just as well for Mr. M'Grath, because a similar itinerant Chartist, who succeeded in calling a meeting at Cottenham a few miles from Cambridge, was so heavily pelted with rotten eggs and other missiles that he had to be rescued by the local policeman. Little more was heard of Chartism in Cambridge.[127] By 1848 the government had weathered the storm, and after the Kennington Common fiasco the *Chronicle* ridiculed 'the mischievous blockheads' who had mismanaged a revolution, the simpletons who had talked themselves into the belief 'that the destiny of this glorious Kingdom was in their dirty hands.'[128] The editorial summary in the *Independent Press* was more penetrating. Chartism, it declared, had been overcome by a combination of its own foolishness and O'Connor's rash leadership. Above all, however, it was overcome by middle-class strength, expecially in the latter's refusal to be intimidated by the threat of physical force.[129]

V

By the terms of the Reform Act of 1832, the county had received an extra Member of Parliament, and over two thousand new voters were added to the electorate. It appeared that the power of the two aristocratic families was finally broken, but as Hatfield discovered, rejoicing proved premature. In December 1832 C.P. Yorke, nephew of the Earl of Hardwicke, was returned, and kept his seat in the thirties and forties.[130] The Yorke family continued to supply a member for the county until 1878. Moreover, he was joined in 1847 by G.J. Manners, third son of the Duke of Rutland, and he held his seat until 1874.[131] The third member was usually a representative of the lesser county families, but it seems that the Chandos clause strengthened, rather than weakened, the hold which the two aristocratic families had on county representation.[132] There also appeared to be a concurrence of opinion between the Whig and Tory county members in these years which was reflected in their criticism of the Malt Tax, their hostility to centralisation, and their determination to uphold the Corn Laws.[133]

The *Chronicle* continued to lend its full support to the agricultural interest and suspected that a government that had weakened on the issue of the secret ballot might also weaken in its defence of the Corn Laws. It tended to see Corn Law opposition as a mixture of religious Dissenters and economic agitators. The Church of England remained to a large extent the church of the landed interest. East Anglia was predominantly agricultural, with little chance of balancing income from agriculture with income from mining or manufactures. Having much less contact with businessmen, bankers, mill-owners and free-trading industrialists than their counterparts in the Midlands and the North, they were less prepared to compromise. In their view even imperfectly operated Corn Laws were better than the unknown dangers of foreign competition.[134] While under the editorship of Weston Hatfield, the *Independent Press* stressed the important connection between corn and currency, maintaining that 'the fluctuations in the currency have tended, more than the Corn Laws themselves, to influence the price and profits of agricultural produce.'[135] Hatfield supported Thomas

Attwood in his campaign to repeal Peel's deflationary Currency Act of 1819, urging that 'The safety of the farmer lies in an increase of the circulating medium . . . The system of the Corn Laws is little else than a delusion', primarily because the benefits of protection were almost negatived by deflation.[136] As early as 1834 he was prepared to accept that some alteration in the Corn Laws was inevitable, but he insisted that relief from the several agricultural burdens should precede the reform.[137] In February 1836 he put forward his plan for agricultural relief. He suggested the commutation of tithes, reform of the rates, the reduction of imports from Ireland and the commutation of the Malt Tax for one on fixed capital.[138] Later he argued for a Corn Law sliding scale, the duty 'diminishing as price rises', but above all he questioned the notion that rural prosperity could only be maintained on the basis of high arable prices.[139] In his opinion farmers could prosper in spite of lower prices if they 'endeavoured to meet foreign competition by adopting newer and more improved methods of cultivation.'[140] If the farmers accepted this change of attitude, it would not be simply a case of political surrender on the part of the landed interest, but an acceptance of changed economic conditions which demanded not protection but increased efficiency and production. Corn Law repeal therefore, to Hatfield, the *Cambridge Advertiser* and later to Peel, became a symbol of social and economic adaptation.[141] The *Chronicle,* as we have seen, accepted the traditional view that high farming could never be a substitute for high prices, and that repeal of the Corn Laws would subvert the traditional structure of rural society.

When the agitation for the repeal of the Corn Laws began in the late thirties, therefore, the *Chronicle* reminded its readers of the dangerous effects repeal would have on a town, county and University which depended almost entirely on income from land, and which possessed no alternative source of income or employment.[142] The primary object of the Manchester Chamber of Commerce and other northern manufacurers who were making such a stir about cheap bread, was 'to reduce the wages of the artisan, in order that they may compete with the foreign manufacturer on better terms.'[143] During meetings held in 1839 the county M.P.s vigorously defended the Corn Laws. The Cambridge and Isle of Ely Farmers' Association was formed to investigate agricultural distress and organise petitions to defend their interests. It was a predominantly Tory organisation and secured the withdrawal of the Whig Townley in 1841 by accusing him of being a free trader. However, some Anti-Corn Law activity continued. In May, Sidney Smith attacked the Corn Laws in a speech delivered at the theatre in Barnwell, and so incited the undergraduates that they proceeded to riot and the proctors had to clear the hall. The *Independent Press* condemned 'the disgraceful conduct' of the students, while the *Chronicle* referred to Smith as 'a travelling Chartist' who merely used the Corn Laws as 'a peg on which to hang the most outrageous attacks on the House of Lords . . . Methodists . . . the clergy and the landed interest' until 'the respectable portion of the house' could bear it no longer.[144] In 1841 three Conservative Members of Parliament were returned for the county, and the *Chronicle* was praised for its efforts on behalf of the landed interest, but the Anti-Corn Law League merely redoubled its efforts and after 1842 concentrated more on the agricultural areas. In 1843 every elector in Cambridge received a package of propaganda material from the League, urging him to vote for Corn Law repeal.[145] Lectures were delivered on the subject at various public houses in Cambridge; John Bright himself visited the town on behalf of the League in 1844 and addressed a meeting behind the Old Greyhound public house in St. Andrew's Street.[146] The *Independent Press* was convinced that the League was about to achieve victory: 'Peel will give free trade as soon as the Anti-Corn Law League are powerful enough to demand it.'[147] It was only a matter of time. Nothing, it appeared, could spur the farmers to action until Peel made an announcement of his intentions.

The *Chronicle,* for its part, continued to defend Peel and reiterated that the farmers and agriculturists were 'wrong in their mistrust of the premier.'[148] Peel, because of the deflationary currency policy he advocated in the 1820s and his granting of Catholic emancipation, had set many farmers and ultra-Tories against him. However, by 1834 the *Chronicle* was prepared to welcome him back.[149] Apart from the fact that there was no real alternative, he had resisted the Whig attack on the Irish Church and remained a staunch supporter of both Church and Constitution in the thirties and early forties. His programme of cautious, moderate reform outlined in the Tamworth Manifesto, the *Chronicle* praised as a policy 'of wisdom, tact and genius.'[150] Peel's policies in finance and on Ireland further emphasised Whig ineptitude. Both the *Independent Press* and the *Advertiser* accepted that Peel was a man of ability, but they also suspected him of being a 'wily partisan', mistrusted by many of his own party.[151] They also noted the hidden element of conflict between Peel, 'the child of cotton and commerce', and the Tory landed aristocracy, and played on Tory fears that Peel 'the Jesuit' would 'succumb to expediency' and betray them again on the issue of the Corn Laws.[152] The Maynooth Grant, which the *Independent Press* welcomed as a measure of justice,[153] reawakened apprehension in the *Chronicle.* Peel, the latter declared, 'is labouring very hard indeed to break to pieces that great party, which placed him in his present lofty position', and few Conservatives now regarded 'the Premier with that trust they so honourably extended to him three years ago.'[154] More ominous was the fact that 'Nobody knows what is to come next. He chooses to shroud himself in mystery.'[155] When the news of the potato blight in Ireland arrived in late 1845, the occasion for repeal which Cobden had prophesied had finally arrived. For this reason the *Chronicle,* many government ministers, and the Tory press in general, refused to accept the reality of the famine - 'week after week it is promised but it never occurs.'[156] Famine in Ireland was relegated to the status of a party question, and its entanglement with Corn Law repeal was to prove a major misfortune for that country. However, the crisis had arrived, and there was no ambiguity now about Peel's intention to suspend the Corn Laws. The *Chronicle* was appalled. Peel 'The grand deluder of 1829 is the grand deluder still',[157] and his scheme for the gradual abolition of the Corn Laws and the opening of the ports was 'comprehensive enough to satisfy the maddest free trader.'[158]

However, Peel's 'package deal' in 1846 was quite acceptable to the editors of the *Independent Press* and the *Cambridge Advertiser* and was in fact similar to the plan advocated by Hatfield in the thirties.[159] It included not only plans for repeal over three years, but also schemes for a drainage loan, cuts in agriculture burdens, and a reduction of import duties on grass and clover seeds, maize and fertilizer. The whole legislative package was designed to encourage farmers to concentrate their hopes on high production instead of high prices. As Peel conceived it, Corn Law repeal was not a means of solving the economic problems of urban society by providing cheap bread, but a means of implementing economic growth.[160] The editor of the *Chronicle,* who was incapable of seeing the measure in such a light, bitterly condemned both the borough and the University representatives for not resigning in protest.[161] However, during the passage of the bill through Parliament he welcomed a new hero for the Tory protectionist cause in Benjamin Disraeli. The editor's attitude to Peel was even less merciful than that of Disraeli. Peel's farewell speech was 'nauseous'; he had committed the cardinal sin, he had grovelled before Cobden.[162] All else was dwarfed 'by the treachery of Peel and his perfidious followers.'[163]

The *Independent Press* was more generous. Although the editor argued that it was too soon to decide whether or not Peel had made a correct decision in repealing the Corn Laws, he insisted that 'Peel was one of the greatest Englishmen of this or any other age.'[164] In an age of revolutions, he had, by his statesmanlike behaviour saved England from revolution. More important, by his recent action he had confirmed the triumph of the middle classes which had been prophesied in 1832: 'By the Reform Bill the predominance of the Middle Classes, in the most active and important branch of our Senate ... was solemnly and irrevocably affirmed. And it is by the Middle Classes that our recent important improvement has been commenced, by *them* has it been sustained, and by *them* has it been carried on, to its final triumph over a reluctant Aristocracy ... The triumph of the Free-trade principle, though a triumph of the people and for the people, has not been a triumph of the populace. We repeat it, it proves the actual existence of that, which it was foretold the Reform Bill would eventually found, the Monarchy of the Middle Classes.'[165]

NOTES AND REFERENCES

1   *Camb. Chron.* 4 Jan. 1833, 2 Jan. 1841; *Camb. Ind. Press* 20 Aug. 1836.
2   *Ibid.* 22 Sept., 2 Nov. 1838, 6 Jan. 1837.
3   *Ibid.* 1 Nov. 1845, *Camb. Ind. Press* 28 Sept. 1833, 1 June 1844.
4   *Ibid.* 22 Aug. 1834, 6 May 1837.
5   Gray, *Cambridge Revisited,* p. 102.
6   *Camb. Chron.* 5 Jan. 1839.
7   *Ibid.* 24 July 1835.
8   *Ibid.* 6 Jan. 1849.
9   Cooper, *Annals* IV, p. 523.

10   *Camb. Ind. Press* 12 Jan. 1833, 4 June 1842, 4 May 1844. See also *Appendix B.*
11   *Ibid.* 19, 26 Mar. 1836. See also Hollis, *Pauper Press,* Ch. 1.
12   *Ibid.* 26 Mar. 1836, 6 May 1837.
13   *Ibid.* 7 Mar. 1835.
14   *Ibid.* 16 May 1835.
15   *Ibid.* 26 Aug. 1837.
16   *Cambridge Guardian* 6, 13 Mar. 1838.
17   *Cambridge General Advertiser* 9 Jan. 1839.
18   *Cambridge Advertiser and Free Press* 31 July 1839 (hereafter abbreviated to *Camb. Adv. and F.P.*).
19   *Camb. Adv. and F.P.* 1 Jan. 1840.
20   *Ibid.* 9 Oct. 1839, 3 July 1844; *Camb. Ind. Press* 4 May 1844.
21   *Cambridge Advertiser and University Herald* 4 Nov. 1846 (hereafter abbreviated to *Camb. Adv. and U.H.*).
22   *Camb. Adv. and F.P.* 31 July 1839.
23   *Ibid.* 8 May 1839.
24   *Ibid.* 2, 16, 23, 30 Oct. 1839.
25   *Ibid.* 15 April 1840, 8 Oct. 1845.
26   *Camb. Adv. and U.H.* 17 Nov. 1847, 28 Mar. 1849, 24 Aug. 1850.
27   *Camb. Adv. and F.P.* 8 May 1839.
28   *Ibid.* 2, 16, 23, 30 Oct. 1839.
29   *Ibid.* 15 April 1840.
30   *Ibid.* 8 Oct. 1845.
31   *Camb. Adv. and U.H.* 17 Nov. 1847, 28 Mar. 1849, 24 Aug. 1850.
32   D. Southgate, *The Passing of the Whigs 1832-86* (1962), p. 37.
33   *Camb. Ind. Press* 15 Oct. 1836, 18 Mar. 1837.
34   *Camb. Chron.* 14, 21, 28 Sept. 1832; see also W.G. Craufurd, *Slavery! Captain Yorke's Views Refuted* (1832).
35   *Camb. Ind. Press* 8, 15 Sept. 1832.
36   *Ibid.* 10 Mar. 1826.
37   *Ibid.* 10 Mar. 1838.
38   *Camb. Chron.* 25 Jan., 12 April 1833.
39   *Ibid.* 21 June 1833.
40   *Ibid.* 3 June 1836, 13 May 1843.
41   *Ibid.* 23 Mar. 1844.
42   *Camb. Ind. Press* 25 June 1836; Read, *Press and People,* p. 123.
43   *Ibid.* 25 June, 9 July 1836.
44   *Ibid.* 16 May 1846.
45   *Ibid.* 6 Dec. 1834.
46   *Camb. Adv. and U.H.* 24 Feb., 17 Mar. 1847.
47   See Fraser, *Evolution of the British Welfare State,* Ch. 2.
48   *Camb. Adv. and F.P.* 7 Aug. 1839; *Camb. Chron.* 16 May 1834.
49   *Camb. Chron.* 24 June 1836. For examples of local resistance, and resentment, in Cambridge see: *Poor Law Commission, Correspondence with Cambs.* PRO. MH.12, 560, 1838-9; *Board of Guardians Minute Books,* G/C/A.Am, Book 7, p. 204; G/Ch./A.Am, Book 1, pp. 315, 369.
50   *Ibid.* 24 June 1836.
51   *Ibid.* 25 Aug. 1838.
52   For organised opposition to the Poor Law see N. Edsall, *The anti-Poor*

Law movement 1834-44 (1971).
53 *Camb. Chron.* 1 Aug. 1834, 8 July 1836; *Camb. Ind. Press* 18 June, 2, 16 July 1836; F.H. Maberly, *To the Poor and their Friends: speeches exhibiting the oppressive nature of the new Poor Law Amendment Act* (1836); *Disturbances and the Poor Law Commission,* PRO. H.O. 52. 28, June, July 1836.
54 Maberly, *To the Poor and their Friends,* p. 11.
55 *Camb. Chron.* 3, 17 June 1836.
56 *Ibid.* 5 Sept. 1834, 3, 18, 24 June 1836, 25 Mar. 1837, 12, 19 Dec. 1846.
57 Maberly, *To the Poor,* p. 8.
58 *Ibid.* p. 8; S.E. Minnis, *A Turbulent Priest* (n.d. but 195-), p. 9; *Disturbances and the Poor Law Commission,* PRO. H.O. 73.51 Aug. 1835; H.O. 52.28 July 1836.
59 *Camb. Chron.* and *Camb. Ind. Press,* 29 July 1837.
60 *Camb. Ind. Press* 29 Oct. 1836, 19 July 1834.
61 *Ibid.* 2 Aug. 1834, 18 June, 2 July 1836, 15 April 1837.
62 *Ibid.* 18 Oct. 1834.
63 *Ibid.* 11 June 1836.
64 *Ibid.* 16 July 1836.
65 *Ibid.* 29 Oct. 1836.
66 *Ibid.* 8 July 1837.
67 *Camb. Chron.* 14 Jan. 1837.
68 *Camb. Ind. Press* 15 April 1837.
69 See *Digested Report of the Evidence taken before the Corporation Commissioners* (1833); *Camb. Chron.* 1 Nov. 1833.
70 *Report of the Evidence,* p. 35.
71 *Camb. Ind. Press* 2, 9 Sept. 1833.
72 *The Times* 16 Nov. 1833. See also Atkinson, *Cambridge Described,* pp. 114-20.
73 *Camb. Chron.* 12 June, 11 Sept. 1835.
74 *Ibid.* 4 Mar. 1836.
75 *Ibid.* 29 April 1837.
76 *Camb. Ind. Press* 1 Sept. 1838.
77 *Ibid.* 20 Oct. 1832.
78 Southgate, *Passing of the Whigs,* p. 40.
79 *Camb. Chron.* 25 Jan. 1833.
80 *Ibid.* 3 April 1841.
81 *Camb. Ind. Press* 11, 18 Feb. 1832, 16, 23 Feb. 1833, 16 Jan. 1836, 1 April 1837.
82 *Camb. Chron.* 18 Mar. 1837.
83 *Camb. Chron.* 21 Mar. 1834.
84 For a full bibliography on this event see A.T. Bartholomew, *Catalogue of the books and papers relating to the University, Town and County of Cambridge, bequeathed by J.W. Clark* (1912), p. 26.
85 J.S. Henslow, *Address to the Reformers of the Town of Cambridge* (1835); *Camb. Ind. Press* 21 June 1834.
86 *Camb. Adv. and F.P.* 4 Sept. 1839, 27 May, 17 June 1840.
87 *Camb. Ind. Press* 15 Aug. 1835.
88 *Camb. Adv. and F.P.* 23 Sept. 1846.
89 *Camb. Chron.* 4 May 1839.

90   *Ibid.* 1 June 1839, 17 June 1843.
91   *Ibid.* 2 June 1838.
92   *Ibid.* 2 Aug. 1833. See also 1 Aug. 1834, 20 Feb., 25 Sept. 1835, 3 Mar. 1838, 4 Sept. 1841, 14 Oct. 1843, 21 June 1845, 29 May 1847.
93   *Ibid.* 8 Mar. 1833.
94   *Camb. Ind. Press* 19 Aug. 1843.
95   *Ibid.* 23 April 1836.
96   *Ibid.* 6 Aug. 1836.
97   *Ibid.* 7 Sept. 1844.
98   *Ibid.* 27 Jan. 1838.
99   Southgate, *Passing of the Whigs,* pp. 91-94.
100   Cooper, *Annals* V, p. 113-24; see also J. Vincent, *Pollbooks: how Victorians voted* (1967).
101   *Camb. Chron.* 13 June 1834, 2 Jan. 1835, 29 July 1837.
102   *Ibid.* 9 Jan. 1835; Pryme, *Recollections,* pp. 201-2.
103   *Camb. Ind. Press* 7 Feb. 1835; J.S. Henslow, *Address to the Reformers of the Town of Cambridge* (1835).
104   *Ibid.* 28 Mar., 25 April 1835; Fawcett, 'Parliamentary Elections in Cambridge' in *P.C.A.S.* ix, (1895), p.167.
105   *Ibid.* 29 April, 6 May 1836.
106   *Ibid.* 31 Aug., 7 Sept. 1839.
107   *Camb. Chron.* 7 Sept. 1839.
108   *Camb. Ind. Press* 29 July 1837. See also Pryme, *Autobiographic Recollections,* pp. 201-2; *Alphabetical List of Cambridge Tradesmen who supported the Conservative Candidate at the Election, 1835; 1837; 1840.*
109   *Camb. Adv. and F.P.* 4, 11 Sept. 1839.
110   *Camb. Chron.* 28 Sept. 1839.
111   *Ibid.* and *Camb. Ind. Press* 18, 25 April 1840.
112   *Ibid.* 18, 25 April 1840.
113   *Ibid.* 18 April 1840.
114   Cooper, *Annals* V, pp. 113-24; *Camb. Chron.* 24 Mar. 1842. For a full account see: *Report of the Commissioners appointed to inquire into the existence of corrupt practices in the Borough of Cambridge,* (1853).
115   *Camb. Ind. Press* 21 Oct. 1837.
116   *Ibid.* 7 Jan. 1837.
117   *Ibid.* 15 July 1837; Pryme, *Autobiographic Recollections,* p. 201.
118   *Ibid.* 15 July 1837.
119   *Ibid.* 4, 11 Feb., 15 July, 2, 23, 30 Sept., 7 Oct., 30 Dec. 1837.
120   *Camb. Chron.* 28 Sept. 1832.
121   *Ibid.* 1 Feb. 1840. See also A. Brown, H. Fearn, R. Young, *Chartism in East Anglia,* W.E.A. Pamphlet (1951).
122   *Camb. Adv. and F.P.* 31 July, 7 Aug. 1839; *Camb. Ind. Press* 15 Dec. 1838.
123   *Camb. Chron.* and *Camb. Ind. Press* May 1841.
124   *Camb. Ind. Press* 16 Nov. 1839, 30 April 1842.
125   Cooper, *Annals* IV pp. 699-700. *Camb. Ind. Press* 1 April 1848.
126   *Camb. Chron.* 8 April 1848.
127   *Ibid.* 8 April 1848.
128   *Ibid.* 15 April 1848.
129   *Camb. Ind. Press* 15 April 1848.

130 For a detailed analysis of Cambridgeshire elections 1826-35 see Moore, *Politics of Deference,* Ch. 2.

131 *Victoria County History,* Cambs. II, p. 418.

132 Moore, *Politics of Deference,* pp. 54, 57-59.

133 *Camb. Chron.* and *Camb. Ind. Press* 1 Feb. 1834, 13 Mar. 1835, 23 Feb. 1839.

134 *Camb. Chron.* 2 Mar. 1836, 21 Feb. 1839.

135 *Camb. Ind. Press* 8 Sept. 1832, 11 Jan. 1834.

136 *Ibid.* 8 Sept. 1832, 2 Mar., 11, 25 May, 13 July 1833.

137 *Ibid.* 1 Feb. 1834.

138 *Ibid.* 13 Feb. 1836.

139 *Ibid.* 26 Jan., 23 Feb. 1839.

140 *Ibid.* 2 Mar. 1839.

141 *Camb. Adv. and F.P.* 8 Oct. 1845. See also D.C. Moore, 'The Corn Laws and High Farming', in *Economic History Review* xviii (1965), p. 545.

142 *Camb. Chron.* 24 Mar. 1838, 23 Mar. 1839, 25 Jan. 1840.

143 *Ibid.* 26 Jan. 1839.

144 Cooper, *Annals* IV, p. 621; *Camb. Ind. Press* and *Camb. Chron.* 18 May 1839.

145 *Camb. Chron.* 11 Mar. 1843.

146 *Ibid.* 6 May 1844.

147 *Camb. Ind. Press* 25 Nov. 1843.

148 *Camb. Chron.* 13, 20 Jan. 1844.

149 *Ibid.* 8 Mar. 1833.

150 *Ibid.* 30 Jan. 1835.

151 *Camb. Ind. Press* 19 June 1841; *Camb. Adv. and F.P.* 25 Dec. 1839.

152 *Ibid.* 19 June 1841; *Camb. Adv. and F.P.* 1 Jan. 1840.

153 *Camb. Ind. Press* 10 May, 5 April 1844.

154 *Camb. Chron.* 5 April 1845.

155 *Ibid.* 19 April 1845.

156 *Ibid.* 8 Nov., 6 Dec. 1845, 28 Mar., 23 May 1846.

157 *Ibid.* 24 Jan. 1846.

158 *Ibid.* 31 Jan. 1846.

159 *Camb. Adv. and F.P.* 28 Jan., 4 Feb. 1846.

160 Moore, 'Corn Laws and High Farming', pp. 544-6, 560.

161 *Camb. Chron.* 7, 21 Feb. 1846.

162 *Ibid.* 23 May, 20 June, 4 July 1846.

163 *Ibid.* 5 Sept. 1846, 6 July 1850.

164 *Camb. Ind. Press* 6 July 1850.

165 *Ibid.* 5 Sept. 1850.

5

The Influence of the Cambridge Press 1780-1850

During the years 1780-1850 the press grew rapidly in power and influence. Cambridge newspapers, from fairly humble beginnings in the early eighteenth century, shared in this expansion. Despite the claim that 'newspapers are the most valuable of all nineteenth-century sources'[1] interest in them has, generally speaking, been mainly confined to their usefulness as a supplementary source of information for other areas of historical research. The history of the newspapers themselves and the lives and opinions of the printers that founded and developed them has been less considered. It remains true, of course, that newspapers offer, and not only to the historian, a wealth of information on a large variety of topics and provide not merely local news and opinion but 'a picture of contemporary life.' In this respect Cambridge newspapers offer a vivid record of social and economic as well as political change during this vital period of transition in English history, and show that the improving spirit of the period was not just the preserve of the industrial Midlands and North.

To place the arguments about the supposed influence of the press in context we need first to define broadly the functions that the newspapers had in nineteenth-century society. First these newspapers were channels of communication. They were one of the means by which people learned what those outside their immediate locality were thinking and doing. They were the quickest means of communicating news of events and opinions to large numbers of people outside a local area. In any period of time people can also read far more than they can learn by word of mouth and, probably more important, the written word enables readers to absorb the content at their own pace. Newspapers were one of the important means of communication by which the members of society related to each other. The power of a newspaper as a means of communication depended on the editor's choice of what to put in and what to leave out. The view of society and events the reader obtained was a product not only of what happened but of constraints on the editor in terms of space, time, cost and of his set of news values. In general the presentation of news and local occurrences in the early nineteenth century was neutral. However, even without an editorial column an editor could give emphasis to news, letters, and opinions he favoured in order to promote his own views. This could be done much more directly by the use of the editorial where an editor could quite explicitly argue a case and comment upon the contents of his news and feature columns. In this way he aimed to shape opinions and influence the reaction of readers to what they read. Newspapers also sought to influence those about *whom* they wrote. Papers 'exposed' scoundrels, politicians, and policies in order to focus attention on them and by bringing pressure to bear upon them, sought to deter, modify, or influence the particular practice, or person, exposed. In all these ways the press could be said to have exercised power in society. It is easier to ask questions than to answer them and the task of evaluating the extent of newspaper influence on Cambridge opinion is a difficult one. Some of the factors involved are complex: sometimes information is not available. Most of the answers must be tentative and exploratory.

By the 1840s the three Cambridge newspapers were together selling approximately 5,000 copies per week.[2] This circulation may seem small by modern standards, but during the early nineteenth century this does not mean that these newspapers therefore had little or no influence. To begin with, many more people read one copy of a newspaper than at present. Newspapers were expensive articles and therefore treated with much care, often being exchanged between friends and neighbours and occasionally given by employer to employee, and thus eventually, if belatedly, finding their way into all sections of the community.[3] The Town Clerk at Tiverton described in a letter how newspapers, including the *Cambridge Intelligencer,* circulated in that area. Having passed through the professional class the final subscriber 'lends it round among the common people.' Another copy circulated through 'fifteen pairs of hands.'[4] The hiring out of newspapers, though illegal, was widely practised. It may be assumed therefore that in this manner each copy would be seen by several families. In Cambridge, customers at public houses, barber shops and coffee houses could expect to find copies available, as well as at the local town newsroom and Mechanics' Institute.[5] As for the rural classes in the county, they found in the village ale-houses a meeting-place where they might hear the news read aloud from one of the local journals.[6] The Cambridge newsroom took 'Four London Papers every day, besides the *Cambridge Chronicle, Independent Press* and *Stamford Mercury* weekly.[7] The latter were also available at the newsroom in Huntingdon and could also be read at 'the Chapter and Peele's Coffee-Houses and at the Auction Mart', in London. By these various means it was estimated that a copy of the *Leeds Mercury* and *Manchester Times* was read, on average, by twenty to twenty-five people.[8] *The Westminster Review* in 1830 calculated that most copies of provincial newspapers were read by seven or eight people.[9]

Readership depended, of course, to a large degree on the literacy range in the local area. One would expect the major buyers of the Cambridge newspapers to be the University and town middle-classes, Dissenters and county gentry, but we must not preclude the possibility of many of the working-classes wanting, and often managing, to acquire newspapers as well. After all, great progress had been made in teaching the lower classes at least to read since the end of the eighteenth century.[10] The working-class reading public was expanding and becoming more diversified in its reading habits as it increased in literacy. There was a whole spectrum of schools for this class by the early nineteenth century, ranging from the humble dame and charity schools to the great experiments of the National, and British and Foreign School, Societies. There were also Sunday schools, workhouse schools and ragged schools, all endeavouring to teach at least the rudiments of reading and writing.[11] As a university town Cambridge was probably better equipped than most as regards education[12] and was full of indirect stimuli, such as ephemeral printing and advertising posters, newspaper broadsheets and election handbills, which offered encouragement and opportunity to practise simple reading. Nor must one forget that this was also the age of self-help and self-education. Reading rooms and small study groups were set up by Mechanics' Institutes, Dissenters, and Trade Union members,[13] and the town could claim its share of all these groups. An estimate therefore of seven or eight readers per newspaper for a fairly literate town such as Cambridge is probably slightly under the true figure and possibly ten or twelve would be nearer the mark.

The newspaper, of course, had to face competition from the London dailies, but in the provinces these were not read to the exclusion of local papers.[14] London papers on the whole were concerned with national politics, London gossip and international affairs and therefore tended to supplement rather than rival the local press, which in Cambridge concentrated on town and county news, University notices and preferments, local politics and important local improvements such as the Eau Brink Cut and the building of railways. Naturally some concession had to be made to national affairs, and so parliamentary debates and extracts from the London papers were featured, but the editors realized that the major task of their newspapers was to report on local affairs.

However, to show that the newspapers achieved a fairly wide circulation in town and county does not in itself prove that the papers exerted much influence on local opinion.[15] The editorial, which was developed as a means of influencing opinion during the period, was basically just an expression of the personal views of the editor, and not a guarantee that these opinions were prevalent. The work of Benjamin Flower illustrates the point very clearly, for although he was based in Cambridge, his circulation pattern shows that most support for his opinions was found in little pockets of Dissenters and radicals spread fairly widely throughout Britain. It is important therefore not to draw conclusions about newspaper influence from studying merely editorial content. Letters, advertisements, circulation patterns and changes in local outlook as expressed in events must also be utilized, if one is to get a balanced impression. It remains true, however, that by the 1830s the main characteristic of most local newspapers was the editorial, as local news and gossip in all the town newpapers tended to be identical - Hatfield, for example, being prepared to admit that he took nearly all of his local gossip from the pages of the rival *Chronicle*.[16]

Some contemporaries firmly believed that the press, and particularly the provincial press, merely reflected opinion.[17] Others maintained that it played a major role in determining opinion.[18] In fact the press was versatile enough to reflect and to guide; 'the press influenced the public but it also mirrored the public.'[19] For many years the *Chronicle* appeared content simply to reflect the predominantly Tory outlook of the town and county, asserting that 'the upper

classes use a Country Paper only for its local news and advertisements, and ...
never dream of attending to the Editor's opinions.'[20] It could be relied upon to
support King and Constitution, Church and University when the need arose.[21]
Secure in its position and patronage it withstood the attempted Tory
reinforcement of *The Huntingdon, Bedford and Cambridge Journal* during the
Catholic emancipation crisis, just as it had ignored the attempt of Flower thirty
years earlier to impel local opinion, in a more radical direction. It had also rejected Flower's method of using the editorial to accomplish his ends, and refused
to take notice of this new political weapon until 1830.

The establishment, and early success, of the *Independent Press* posed a more
serious threat to its position, and under the editorship of Brown the *Chronicle*
was soon using an editorial which was every bit as vigorous as that of its rival. Up
to this time, however, it gave an impression of complacency - its appeal was
to the converted and convinced. After 1830 it appeared to find the new competition difficult to master and had to struggle to maintain merely its position. On
many of the less central political issues, for example currency inflation and
taxation, it became much less dogmatic, maintaining that 'it is sufficient if we
suggest matter for reflection, and leave the decision to the intelligence and good
sense of our readers.'[22] Although it is now more obviously on the defensive, and
less sure of its position after the Reform Act of 1832, its support for the basic
principles of Toryism never wavered and it is only with reluctance that it accepted
Peel's more moderate policy of Conservatism in the thirties. On the other hand,
although the *Cambridge Intelligencer,* and the *Independent Press,* could count
on some support, they had to cultivate reform opinion if they were to survive.
The *Intelligencer* from 1793 to 1803 barely accomplished this, mainly because
of the extent of its national circulation. It was much more than a local paper,
and for that very reason it lacked security. It was the product of a particular
period and of special circumstances, and proved unique in many ways, but what
influence it had was probably as much national as local. The *Intelligencer* was
one of the first provincial newspapers to try to educate and shape public opinion,
but it would be difficult to measure its impact on opinion at the national level.
At the turn of the nineteenth century it was the only provincial newspaper in
the country which denounced the war with France as unjust and materially
ruinous. It led the reform assault on political corruption in borough and county
as well as advocating religious liberty in England and Ireland. These policies
were all eventually taken up and developed by Weston Hatfield in the 1820s and
1830s.

The commercial roots of the *Independent Press* were much more firmly
planted in the local area. It was a well-printed and commercially produced
newspaper and, working from a sound basis of support for Dissenters, moderate
reformers and those interested in Fen affairs, it soon built up a substantial
readership.[23] Though it gradually became more overtly radical, it managed to
retain the support of the local Whigs. Its links with the Whig party were strong —
George Pryme becoming one of the trustees early in the 1820s when the newspaper was trying to establish itself — but its editorials constantly urged the
Whigs to be more progressive, enlightened and reformist. Hatfield was not afraid

to risk hostile public or party reaction, fully accepting that it was 'the duty of an editor of a public journal . . . to give his opinion on all public questions.'[24] On the controversial Irish problem, for example, he argued that it was imperative that England began to remodel its opinions respecting Ireland[25] and grant emancipation, which was never merely a religious but 'a civil right.'[26] Though based in an agricultural county, he continually drew attention to the problems of the industrial North and both accepted and preached the doctrine of Free Trade. On the issue of the Corn Laws he was prepared 'to incur the risk of giving offence to a considerable body of our subscribers' yet he continued to advocate a policy of high farming rather than protection.[27]

Its success as a newspaper may well indicate that the *Independent Press* had some considerable influence on the shaping of public opinion.[28] Some of this was obviously due to the gradual change in general political outlook manifested in the twenties, but some credit must also be given to the vigorous quality of its editorial writing. The fact that a second liberal newspaper, *The Cambridge Advertiser and Free Press*, was established and survived in the town in the 1840s is some indication of how far Flower and Hatfield were successful in forming and educating reform opinion. On major reform questions, both local and national, the *Independent Press* stimulated political awareness by encouraging debate and discussion. Hatfield used the editorial to persuade local people to embark on political agitation, and once launched used his newspaper as an organ of publicity for them.

In this way the power of the platform was enormously extended by the contribution of the press during the period. County meetings, petitions, election speeches and events were fully reported, usually accompanied by editorial comments.[29] The results are described by Croker in a letter to Peel in 1822: 'The cause of reform, it cannot be doubted, has made great progress; public opinion is created by the Press or by public meetings . . . . Now, almost the whole Press and all public meetings are loud for reform . . .'[30] The press up to 1846 was a far more important instrument of progress and reform than the platform, and even the Anti-Corn Law League owed much of its success as a propagandist organisation to its use of newspapers, tracts and pamphlets.[31] Results were not expected quickly. Years of steady editorial writing was essential before any changes were noticeable. Repetition of argument was vital. J.A. Roebuck wrote of the influence of newspapers:

> The powers and opportunities of a teacher of the people through the periodical Press, is greater than any other class of teachers . . . [for] by constant repetition, he is able to produce a certain lasting effect. New ideas cannot be introduced by a sudden or singular effort, however powerful or well directed; it is the dropping of the water on the stone, the precept upon precept, that brings about important changes. The people can be effectually moved only by being constantly addressed.[32]

We have already seen how Flower spent ten, and Hatfield twenty, years in their efforts to rouse local opinion and stimulate action on the issue of reform. Unlike Hodson they were prepared to challenge what could be regarded as widely held opinions in town and county, i.e. support for Pitt's repressive domestic policy, the waging of war against France, Catholic emancipation and the Corn Laws. Through the resultant conflict of opinion and the dissemination of new ideas public opinion gradually became more responsive. The reading public in Cambridge had an advantage over that of many other towns, as it possessed a Tory and a radical newspaper from a comparatively early date.[33]

By the 1830s, then, both newspapers in Cambridge were lively, interesting and responsible organs of opinion, capable of making excellent use of the editorial as a means of influencing, guiding or shaping public ideas and attitudes. However, whereas the *Independent Press* displayed an interest in both local affairs and major national issues, the overwhelming characteristic of the *Chronicle* was its Tory parochialism and commitment to the status quo. This can be seen as one of its strengths, as it never changed its outlook and thereby sustained weaker loyalties through the difficult reform years after 1832, when Tory fortunes and morale were low. Nevertheless it was the radical liberal press in Cambridge that enjoyed the satisfaction of success as most of the policies it advocated — religious and political freedom, Free Trade and Corporation reform — were adopted by Parliament and accepted by the people. Theirs was neither an easy nor a popular task. Both Flower and Hatfield suffered from legal as well as social and political hostility. It was no more than they expected. They had dared to introduce radical and liberal opinions into a traditionally Tory area and had worked and suffered for what success and influence they had achieved. It was no more than they deserved.

NOTES AND REFERENCES

1   A. Briggs, *Economic History Review,* vii (1954), p. 254.
2   See *Appendix B.*
3   A. Aspinall, 'The Circulation of Newspapers in the early nineteenth-century' in *Review of English Studies* xii (1946), pp. 35-6; R.K. Webb, *The British Working Class Reader 1790-1848* (1955), Ch. 1.
4   Chalk, 'Circulation of Newspapers', *Notes and Queries,* vol. 169, p. 336.
5   *Camb. Chron.* 19 June 1835; *Camb. Ind. Press* 1 Mar. 1845.
6   Aspinall, 'Circulation of Newspapers', p. 37.
7   *Camb. Chron.* 5 Jan. 1827, 15 April 1836.
8   Read, *Press and People,* p. 202.
9   Aspinall, 'Circulation of Newspapers', p. 30.
10 R.K. Webb, 'Working-Class Readers in Early Victorian England' in *English Historical Review,* LXV (1950), p. 350. Stone, 'Literacy in England in *Past and Present* (1969), p. 137.
11 R.K. Webb, 'The Victorian Reading Public' in *University Quarterly* xii, (1957), pp.31-2.
12 See *Victoria County History, Cambs.* II, (1948), pp. 345-52.
13 Webb, *British Working Class Reader,* p. 20.

14   Read, *Press and People,* p. 203.
15   L.M. Salmon, *The Newspaper and the Historian* (1923), p. 252.
16   *Camb. Ind. Press* 24 Jan. 1829.
17   Aspinall, *Politics and the Press,* p. 5
18   Salmon, *op. cit.* pp. 253-54.
19   A. Briggs, 'Press and Public in early nineteenth century Birmingham', *Dugdale Society Occasional Papers,* No. 8 (1949), p. 6.
20   *Camb. Chron.* 9 Sept. 1831.
21   *Camb. Ind. Press* 2 April 1831.
22   *Camb. Chron.* 22 Jan. 1836.
23   Mitchell, *Newspaper Directory,* p. 124.
24   *Camb. Ind. Press* 2 April 1831.
25   *Ibid.* 19 Aug. 1843.
26   *Ibid.* 28 Nov. 1845.
27   *Ibid.* 16 May 1835.
28   See *Appendix B.*
29   H. Jephson, *The Platform; its Rise and Progress,* I, (1892), p. 18.
30   *Ibid.* quoted, I, p. 568.
31   Aspinall, 'Circulation of Newspapers' p. 43.
32   Quoted by Jephson, *The Platform,* II, pp. 602-3.
33   See Read, *Press and People,* pp. 72-3, 82, 90, 93.

APPENDIX A

List of Cambridge Newspapers 1744-1850

1. *Cambridge Journal and Weekly Flying Post,* 1744–1767
   Printers: R. Walker and T. James,   1744–1753
                  T. James,   1753–1758
                  S. James,   1758–1767
   Proprietors: As above
   Politics: Neutral – Tory
   Location: Cambridge University Library, 1745–1766.
                 (Broken selection, mostly concentrated in the years 1746–1769)
                 British Museum Colindale 1746, 1751–1753, 1755–1760. (Broken selection, very imperfect)
                 Cambridgeshire Collection, Central Library, Cambridge. (Six issues only)

2. *Cambridge Chronicle,* 1762–1767.
   Printers: T. Fletcher and F. Hodson,   1762–1767
   Proprietors: As above
   Politics: Neutral – Tory
   Location: Cambridge University Library, 1762–1767
                 Cambridgeshire Collection, Cambridge, 1762–1767

3. *Cambridge Chronicle and Journal,* 1767–1812
   Cambridge Chronicle and Journal and Huntingdonshire Gazette, 1812–1849
   Cambridge Chronicle and University Journal, 1849–1934
   Printers: T. Fletcher and F. Hodson,   1767–1778
                  F. Hodson,   1778–1812
                  J. Hodson,   1812–1832
                  F. Hodson and C.E. Brown,   1832–1837
                  C.E. Brown,   1837–1849
                  C.W. Naylor,   1849–1878
   Proprietors: As above
   Politics: Tory, ultra-Tory
   Location: Cambridge University Library, 1767–1934
                 British Museum Colindale, 1793–1795, 1796–1812 (very imperfect), 1812–1934

Cambridgeshire Collection, Cambridge 1770–1934
Cambridgeshire County Record Office, 1812–1843 (imperfect)
St John's College Library, Cambridge, 1772–1774 (very imperfect), 1775–1776, 1786–1787, 1789–1808, 1821–1840, 1850–1856

4. *Cambridge Intelligencer*, 1793–1803
   Printers: B. Flower, 1793–1803
   Proprietors: R. Flower 'and certain other Liberal gentlemen'
   Politics: Radical
   Location: Cambridge University Library, 1793–1803
                British Museum Colindale 1793–1797, 1797–1800 (imperfect)
                Cambridgeshire Collection, 1793–1803

5. *Huntingdon Bedford Peterborough and Cambridge Gazette*, 1813–1819
   *Huntingdon Bedford and Peterborough Gazette and Cambridge and Hertford
       Independent Press*, 1819–1839
   Cambridge Independent Press, 1839–1934
   Cambridge Independent Press and Chronicle, 1934–
   Printers: W. Hatfield,   1813–1837
                J. Hatfield,   1837–1841
                H. Smith,   1841–1866
                W.J. Hatfield,   1866–1871
   Proprietors: Jones, Hatfield, Twigg and Co., 1813–1824. Certain Whig noblemen and gentlemen, 1824–1841, represented by four trustees, namely, Wm. Hatfield, G. Pryme, S. Wells and F. Eaden.
                H. Smith, 1841–1866
   Politics: Radical – Whig
   Location: Cambridge University Library, 1859–1934
                British Museum Colindale, 1818–1819, 1825–1934
                Cambridgeshire Collection, Cambridge, 1815–1829, 1831–1837, 1839–1853, 1856–.
                Cambridgeshire County Record Office, 1837–1844 (very imperfect)

6. *Huntingdon Bedford and Cambridge Weekly Journal*, 1825–1828
   Printers: A.P. Wood,   1825–1826
                H.G. James,   1827–1828
   Proprietors: H.G. James, 1825–1828
   Politics: ultra-Tory
   Location: British Museum Colindale, 1825–1828

7. *Cambridge Guardian*, 1838
   Printers: S. Wilson and E. Wade,   1838
   Proprietors: As above

Politics: Liberal — Whig
Location: British Museum Colindale, 1838 (2 copies only)

8. *Cambridge General Advertiser*, 1839
   Cambridge Advertiser and Free Press, 1839—1846
   Cambridge Advertiser and University Herald, 1846—1850

Printers:	W. Metcalfe and J. Palmer,	1839
	W. Warwick and W. Metcalfe,	1839—1846
	W. Cannon,	1846—1847
	J. Caton,	1847—1849
	J. Dickie,	1849—1850
	T. Kennedy,	1850

Proprietors: 'Resident gentlemen' 1839—1846
As above 1846—1850
Location   British Museum Colindale, 1839—1850
Cambridgeshire Collection, Cambridge 1839—1850
(imperfect)
Cambridgeshire County Record Office 1841—1847
(very imperfect, 42 copies only).

APPENDIX B

Circulation of Cambridge Newspapers
1764-1850

There are two main sources of information on newspaper circulation in the early nineteenth century. The first is from statements made by the newspapers themselves, which are outlined below up to 1833, and the second is the 'House of Commons Accounts and Papers' listed in *The New Cambridge Bibliography of English Literature* (Cambridge, 1969), III, 1785-1787. These are the official returns of the number of newspaper stamps issued and are available for the years 1832-33 and 1835-55. Especially useful for Cambridge newspapers are:

Year	Volume	No. of Paper	Page
1833	XXXII	569	614
1836	XLV	388	357
1837	XXXIX	526	305
1843	XXX	174	543
1851	XVII	558	546-7

Newspaper Circulation to 1833

	1764[1]	1793[2]	1797[2]	1798[2]	1833[3]
1. *Cambridge Intelligencer*	–	650	2700	2000	–
2. *Cambridge Independent Press*	–	–	–	–	1700[3]
3. *Huntingdon Bedford and Cambridge Weekly Journal*	–	–	–	–	–
4. *Cambridge Journal*	1000	–	–	–	–
5. *Cambridge Chronicle and Journal*	–	–	–	–	–

[1] *Cambridge Journal* amalgamated with the *Cambridge Chronicle* 1767. Estimate of 1000 based on the editorial claim that 600 weekly sent to one town in the County of Lincoln. *Cambridge Chronicle* 1 Sept. 1764.

[2] *Cambridge Intelligencer* 6 Jan. 1798.

[3] *Cambridge Independent Press* 12 Jan. 1833.

NEWSPAPER CIRCULATION 1833–50[1]

	1833	1834	1835[2]	1836	1837	1838	1839	1840	1841
1 CAMBRIDGE ADVERTISER, and Free Press.	—	—	—	—	—	—	45,500	34,500	37,000
							875	680	725
2 CAMBRIDGE CHRONICLE and Journal.	55,050	—	(60,200)[2]	70,250	71,608	71,550	79,250	86,100	86,000
	1,100		1,200	1,400	1,430	1,430	1,580	1,720	1,720
3 CAMBRIDGE INDEPENDENT PRESS.	95,000	—	(72,000)[2]	84,225	115,500	115,000	108,000	121,188	115,000
	1,700		1,450	1,680	2,300	2,298	2,160	2,400	2,298
4 TOTAL WEEKLY AVERAGE NEWSPAPER SALE			(2,650)[2]	3,080	3,730	3,728	4,515	4,800	4,743

	1842	1843	1844	1845	1846	1847	1848	1849	1850
1 CAMBRIDGE ADVERTISER,[3] and Free Press.	37,000	36,000	36,000	34,125	36,900	36,550	35,000	25,000	8,150
	725	705	705	675	723	718	690	490	155
2 CAMBRIDGE CHRONICLE and Journal.	89,750	89,175	86,500	85,950	85,250	87,000	80,700	96,550	105,100
	1,795	1,783	1,730	1,720	1,700	1,735	1,610	1,900	2,100
3 CAMBRIDGE INDEPENDENT PRESS.	116,000	110,000	123,000	128,500	121,000	127,500	126,000	138,000	121,000
	2,318	2,200	2,260	2,550	2,410	2,545	2,520	2,750	2,410
4 TOTAL WEEKLY AVERAGE NEWSPAPER SALE.	4,838	4,685	4,695	4,945	4,833	4,998	4,820	5,140	4,665

[1] Two totals are given in each year, the number of stamps issued and an approximate weekly average.
[2] Estimate based on figures for July 1835 – December 1835. See House of Commons, Accounts and Papers (1836), XLV, p.357.
[3] Cambridge Advertiser and University Herald from 1846–50.

APPENDIX C

Stamp Duty on Newspapers
1789-1853

Newspaper Stamp Duty 1789–1855

Year	Newspaper stamp duty	Advertisement duty (each)	Price of the *Cambridge Chronicle*
1789	2d	3s	3½d
1797	3½d	3s	6d
1815	4d	3/6d	7d
1833	4d	1/6d	7d
1836	1d	1/6d	4½d
1853	1d	abolished	5d
1855	abolished		4d

SELECT BIBLIOGRAPHY

The main sources used in the writing of this book have been the 5000 or so newspapers listed in *Appendix A*, which should be treated as part of the bibliography. Books by the same author are listed chronologically.

I.   Manuscript Authorities

Hardwicke Papers: *Additional Manuscripts* 35392-35394,35424. *Supplementary Manuscripts* 45040.

Home Office: *Letters and Papers* 42/26-71; *Domestic Entry Books* 43/4-13; *Law Officers' Reports* 119/1; *Secret Papers/Dissenters* 123/XIX; *Treasury Solicitors' Letters* 24/3/88; *Disturbances and the Poor Law Commission* H.O. 52.28; 73.51; *Poor Law Commission Correspondence with Cambs.* M.II. 12.560.

Place Papers: *Additional Manuscripts* 27818.

II.   Parliamentary Papers

Hansard: *Accounts and Papers* (1833) XXXII, 569; (1836) XLV, 388; (1837) XXIX, 526; (1843) XXX, 174; (1851) XVII, 558.

Reports: *Report on the Charities of Cambridgeshire, 1839. Select Committee on Cambridge Borough Petition, 1840.*
Report of the Commissioners appointed to inquire into the existence of corrupt practices in the Borough of Cambridge, 1853.

III. Public Records

Cambridgeshire County
Record Office: *BOARD OF GUARDIANS MINUTE BOOKS*
G/C/A.AM, Cambridge Union 1836-41;
G/Ch/A.AM, Chesterton Union 1836-41

IV. Books and Articles: General

Adams, L.P.	*Agricultural Depression and Farm Relief in England 1813-1852,* London, 1932.
Adams, M.R.	*Studies in the Literary Backgrounds of English Radicalism,* Lancaster, 1947.
Adams, Sarah Flower	*Vivia Perpetua: a dramatic poem in five acts. With a memoir of the author,* London, 1893.
Allen, C.J.	*The Great Eastern Railway,* London, 1955.
Allnutt, W.H.	'English Provincial Presses III', in *Bibliographica* II, 1896.
Andrews, A.	*The History of British Journalism,* 2 vols., London, 1859.
Armytage, W.H.G.	'The Editorial Experiences of Joseph Gales 1786-94', in *North Carolina Historical Review,* XXVIII, 1951.
Ashworth, W.	*The Genesis of Modern British Town Planning,* London, 1954.
Aspinall, A.	'The Circulation of Newspapers in the early nineteenth century', in *Review of English Studies* (XXII), 1946.
"	'Statistical Accounts of London Newspapers during the Eighteenth century', in *English Historical Review,* 1948.
"	*Politics and the Press c.1780-1854,* London, 1949.
Asquith, I.	'Advertising and the Press in the late eighteenth and early nineteenth centuries', in *Historical Journal,* XVIII, 1975.
Best, F.G.A.	'The Religious Difficulties of National Education in England 1800-1870', in *Cambridge Historical Journal,* XII, 1956.
"	'The Protestant Constitution and its

	Supporters', in *Transactions of the Royal Historical Society,* 5th Series, vol. 8, 1958.
Black, E.C.	*The Association: British extraparliamentary political organisation 1769-93,* Cambridge, Mass., 1963.
Bourne, H.R. Fox	*English Newspapers,* 2 vols., London, 1887.
Briggs, A.	'Press and Public in early nineteenth century Birmingham', *Dugdale Society Occasional Papers,* No. 8, Oxford, 1949.
"	*The Age of Improvement,* London, 1959.
"	*Victorian Cities,* London, 1963.
Brock, M.	*The Great Reform Act,* London, 1973.
Brown, P.A.	*The French Revolution in English History,* London, 1918.
Caird, J.	*English Agriculture in 1850-51,* London, 1852.
Cannon, J.	*Parliamentary Reform 1640-1842,* Cambridge, 1973.
Cartwright, Major J.	*The Life and Correspondence,* ed. F.D. Cartwright, 2 vols., London, 1826.
Chalk, E.S.	'Circulation of XVIII-Century Newspapers', in *Notes and Queries,* vol. 169, 1935.
Chambers, J.D. and Mingay, G.E.	*The Agricultural Revolution 1750-1880,* London, 1966.
Clark, D.M.	*British Opinion and the American Revolution,* New Haven, Conn., 1930.
Coleman, D.C.	*The British Paper Industry 1495-1860,* Oxford, 1958.
Collet, C.D.	*The History of the Taxes on Knowledge,* London, 1899.
Cowherd, R.G.	*The Politics of English Dissent,* New York, 1956.
Cranfield, G.A.	*A Handlist of English Provincial Newspapers and Periodicals 1700-1760,* Cambridge Bibliographical Society Monograph No. 2, Cambridge, 1952.
"	'Additions and Corrections', in *Cambridge Bibliographical Society* II, 1956.

Cranfield, G.A.	*The Development of the Provincial Newspaper 1700-1760,* Oxford, 1962.
Croker, J.W.	*Correspondence and Diaries,* (ed.) Jennings, L.J., London, 1884.
Darby, H.C.	*The Draining of the Fens,* Cambridge, 1940.
Defoe, D.	*A Tour thro' the whole island of Great Britain,* 3 vols., London, 1724-27.
	Dictionary of National Biography, London, 1908.
Donnelly, F.K. and Baxter, J.L.	'Sheffield and the English Revolutionary Tradition 1791-1820', in *International Review of Social History* XX, 1975.
Dunbabin, J.D.	*Rural discontent in nineteenth-century Britain,* London, 1974.
Edsall, N.C.	*The anti-Poor Law movement 1833-44,* Manchester, 1971.
Fay, C.R.	*The Corn Laws and Social England,* Cambridge, 1932.
Ford, T.	*The Compositor's Handbook,* London, 1854.
Fraser, D.	*The Evolution of the British Welfare State,* London, 1973.
Gordon, D.I.	*A Regional History of the Railways of Great Britain: The Eastern Counties,* vol. 5, London, 1968.
Gow, H.	*The Unitarians,* London, 1928.
Grant, J.	*The Newspaper Press: its origin, progress and present position,* 3 vols., London, 1871-2.
Henriques, U.	*Religious Toleration in England 1787-1833,* London, 1961.
Hinkhouse, F.J.	*The Preliminaries of the American Revolution as seen in the English Press 1763-75,* New York, 1926.
Hobsbawm, E.J. and Rudé, G.	*Captain Swing,* London, 1969.
Hollis, P.	*The Pauper Press: A study in working class radicalism of the 1830s,* Oxford, 1970.
Holt, R.V.	*The Unitarian Contribution to Social Progress in England,* London, 1938.

Howe, E.	*The London Compositor,* London, 1947.
Hunt, F.K.	*The Fourth Estate,* London, 1850.
Innis, H.A.	'The Newspaper in Economic Development' in *Journal of Economic History Supplement,* December 1942.
Jephson, H.	*The Platform: its Rise and Progress,* 2 vols., London, 1892.
Kitson-Clark, G.S.R.	'The Repeal of the Corn Laws', in *Economic History Review,* 2nd Series IV, 1951.
Knight, C.	*The Old Printer and the Modern Press,* London, 1854.
Lincoln, A.	*Some Political and Social Ideas of English Dissent,* Cambridge, 1938.
Machin, G.I.T.	*The Catholic Question in English Politics 1820-30,* Oxford, 1964.
McKeown, T. and Brown, R.G.	'Reasons for the decline in mortality in the nineteenth century', in *Population Studies,* 16, 1962.
McLachlan, H. (ed.)	*Letters of Theophilus Lindsey,* Manchester, 1920.
"	*The Unitarian Movement in the Religious Life of England,* London, 1934.
Merle, G.	'The Provincial Newspaper Press', in *Westminster Review* XII, 1830.
Mineka, F.E.	*The Dissidence of Dissent: the Monthly Repository 1806-1838,* Chapel Hill, N.C., 1944.
Mitchell, C.	*Newspaper Press Directory,* London, 1856.
Moore, D.C.	'The Corn Laws and High Farming', in *Economic History Review,* 2nd Series XVIII, 1965.
"	*The Politics of Deference,* Hassocks, Sussex, 1976.
Morrison, S.	'The Bibliography of Newspapers and the writing of History', in *The Library,* Series V, IX, 1954.
"	*The English Newspaper,* Cambridge, 1932.
Moxon, J.	*Mechanick Exercises on the Whole Art of*

	Printing 1683-4, (ed.) Davis, H. and Carter, H., London, 1962.
Musson, A.E.	'Newspaper Printing in the Industrial Revolution', in *Economic History Review,* Second Series X, 1957-8.
O'Brien, C.C. and Vanech, W.D.	*Power and Consciousness,* London, 1969.
Orwin, C.S. and C.S.	*The Open Fields,* Oxford, 1938.
Partington, C.F.	*The Printer's Complete Guide,* London, 1825.
Patterson, A. Temple	*Radical Leicester,* Leicester, 1954.
Rea, R.R.	*The English Press in Politics 1760-74,* Lincoln, Nebr., 1963.
Read, D.	'John Harland: the Father of Provincial Reporting', in *Manchester Review,* vol. 8, 1958.
"	*Press and People 1790-1850: opinion in three English cities,* London, 1961.
"	*The English Provinces c. 1760-1960: a study in influence,* London, 1964.
Robinson, H. Crabb	*Diary, Reminiscences and Correspondence of Henry Crabb Robinson,* ed. Sadler, T., 2 vols., London, 1872.
Rudé, G.	*Wilkes and Liberty: a social study of 1763 to 1774,* Oxford, 1962.
Salmon, L.M.	*The Newspaper and the Historian,* New York 1923.
Southgate, D.G.	*The Passing of the Whigs 1832-86,* London, 1962.
Stephenson, H.W.	*The Author of Nearer, my God, to Thee,* London, 1922.
Stone, L.	'Literacy and Education in England 1640-1900', in *Past and Present,* 42, 1969.
Stromberg, R.N.	*Religious liberalism in eighteenth-century England,* Oxford, 1954.
Thompson, D.M. (ed.)	*Nonconformity in the nineteenth century,* London, 1972.
Thompson, E.P.	*The Making of the English Working Class,*

London, 1963.

Times Tercentenary Handlist of English and Welsh Newspapers, London, 1920.

Timperley, C.H.   *A Dictionary of Printers and Printing,* London, 1839.

"   *Encyclopaedia of Literary and Typographical Anecdote,* London, 1842.

Vincent, J.R.   *Pollbooks: how Victorians voted,* Cambridge, 1967.

Wadsworth, A.P.   'Newspaper Circulations 1800-1954', in *Transactions of the Manchester Statistical Society,* 1954-5.

Ward, W.R.   *Religion and Society in England 1790-1850,* London, 1972.

Watson, G.   *The New Cambridge Bibliography of English Literature,* vol. 1–, Cambridge, 1969–.

Webb, R.K.   'Working Class Readers in Early Victorian England', in *English Historical Review,* LXV, 1950.

"   *The British Working Class Reader 1790-1848,* London, 1955.

"   'The Victorian Reading Public', in *Universities Quarterly,* vol. 12, 1957.

Wickwar, W.H.   *The Struggle for the Freedom of the Press 1819-1832,* London, 1928.

Wiles, R.M.   *Freshest Advices: Early Provincial Newspapers in England,* Ohio, 1965.

Williams, G.A.   *Artisans and sans-culottes: popular movements in France and Britain during the French Revolution,* London, 1968.

Wyvill, C.   *Political Papers,* York, 1804.

Young, A.   *Annals of Agriculture, and other useful arts,* 46 vols., London, 1784-1808.

V.   Books and Articles: Cambridge

Many of these books, tracts and so on, are to be found listed in the *Cam Catalogues* of the Cambridge University Library and the *Cambridgeshire Collection* in the Central Library, Cambridge.

Three useful bibliographies are:

Bartholomew, A.T.   *Catalogue of the books and papers relating to the Town and County of Cambridge, bequeathed by J.W. Clark,* Cambridge, 1912.

Bowes, R.   *A catalogue of books printed at or relating to the University, Town and County of Cambridge from 1521 to 1893,* Cambridge, 1894.

Dring, W.E.   *The Fen and the Furrow: books on South Cambridgeshire and the Fenland,* Cambridge, 1974.

       *   *   *

    Abstract of the Evidence given in support of the London and Cambridge Junction Canal Bill, before a committee of the House of Commons, London, 1812.

Ackermann, R.   *A History of the University of Cambridge,* 2 vols., London, 1815.

    Alphabetical List of the Cambridge Tradesmen who supported the Conservative Candidate at the Election, 1835; 1837; 1840.

Atkinson, T.D.   *Cambridge Described and Illustrated, with an introduction by J.W. Clark,* London, 1897.

Beverley, J.   *The Trial of William Frend,* Cambridge, 1793.

Beverley, R.M.   *A letter to His Royal Highness the Duke of Gloucester, Chancellor, on the present corrupt state of the University of Cambridge,* London, 1833.

    Boro'mongers Chronicle; or Corporation Purge, Cambridge, 1831.

Bowes, R.   'On the First and Other Cambridge Newspapers', in *Proceedings of the Cambridge Antiquarian Society* (VIII), 1895.

Bury, J.P.T.   *J. Romilly's Cambridge Diary 1832-42, selected passages,* Cambridge, 1967.

Cam, H.   'John Mortlock III, Master of the Town of Cambridge', in *Proceedings of the Cambridge Antiquarian Society* (XL), 1939-42.

Cantabrigia Depicta, A Concise and Accurate Description of the University and Town of Cambridge, Cambridge, 1781.

Carter, E.   *The History of the County of Cambridge,* London, 1819. (First edition 1753).

Cooper, C.H.   *Annals of Cambridge,* Cambridge, 5 vols., 1842-1908.

"   *Memorials of Cambridge,* Cambridge, 3 vols., 1860-66.

Corporation Cambridge Chronicle and Journal and Humbugboro Gazette, Cambridge, 1829.

Cradock, P.   *The Cambridge Union,* Cambridge, 1953.

Cranfield, G.A.   'The First Cambridge Newspaper', in *Proceedings of the Cambridge Antiquarian Society* (XLV), 1952.

Craufurd, G.W.   *Slavery! Captain Yorke's Views Refuted,* Cambridge, 1832.

Description(s) of the University, Town and County of Cambridge, Cambridge, 1785, 1790, 1796.

Digested Report of the Evidence taken before the Corporation Commissioners, Cambridge, 1833.

Fawcett, W.M.   'Parliamentary Elections at Cambridge', in *Proceedings of the Cambridge Antiquarian Society* (IX), 1895.

Fellows, R.B.   'Railways to Cambridge, Actual and Projected', in *Proceedings of the Cambridge Antiquarian Society* (XLII), 1949.

"   *Railways to Cambridge, actual and proposed,* Cambridge, 1976. (Reprinted from the original edition of 1948.)

Flower, B.   *The French Constitution,* London, 1792.

"   *National Sins Considered, in two letters to the Rev. T. Robinson,* Cambridge, 1796.

"   *The proceedings of the House of Lords in the Case of Benjamin Flower,* Cambridge, 1800.

Flower, B.   *An Address to the Freeholders of Cambridge-shire on the General Election,* Cambridge, 1802.

"   *Divine Judgement on Guilty Nations: a discourse to Protestant Dissenters,* Cambridge, 1804.

"   *Flower's Political Review and Monthly Register,* Harlow, 1807-10.

"   *Statement of the Facts,* Harlow, 1808.

"   *Obituary,* by W.J. Fox in *The Monthly Repository New Series,* vol. III, 1829.

Flower, E.   *Obituary,* in *The Monthly Repository New Series,* vol. V, 1810.

Frend, W.   *Peace and Union Recommended,* St. Ives, 1793.

"   *An Account of the proceedings in the University of Cambridge against William Frend,* Cambridge, 1793.

Gooch, W.   *General View of the Agriculture of the County of Cambridge,* London, 1811-13.

Gray, A.   *Cambridge and its story,* London, 1912.

"   *The Town of Cambridge; a history,* Cambridge, 1925.

Gray, A. and Brittain, F.   *A history of Jesus College Cambridge,* London, 1960.

Gray, A.B.   'John Bowtell, Bookbinder and Antiquary 1753-1815', in *Cambridge Antiquarian Society Communications* (XI), 1903-6.

"   *Cambridge Revisited,* Cambridge, 1921, (reprinted 1974).

Gunning, H.   *Reminiscences of the University, Town and County of Cambridge,* 2 vols., London, 1854.

Hampson, E.M.   *The Treatment of Poverty in Cambridge-shire 1597-1834,* Cambridge, 1934.

Hardwicke, Philip Yorke, 3rd Earl of,   *Observations upon the Eau Brink Cut; with a proposal,* London, 1793.

Hardwicke, Philip Yorke, 3rd Earl of,   *The inutility to the South level of the intended new channel from Eau Brink to Lynn... a letter to the Earl of Hardwicke by a South Level Proprietor,* King's Lynn, 1793.

Hatfield, W.   *Petition of Weston Hatfield, Printer, of Cambridge, complaining of undue influence at the Election for Cambridge,* London, 1820.

"   *The Trial and Acquittal of Mr. Weston Hatfield, on a false charge of riot and misdemeanor,* Cambridge, 1820.

"   *A Full Report of the Important Toll Cause of Brett vs. Beales,* Cambridge, 1826.

Henslow, J.S.   *Address to the Reformers of the Town of Cambridge,* Cambridge, 1835.

Hodson, J.   *The Cambridge Election,* Cambridge, 1819.

Humfrey, C.   *A Report upon the present state of the River Cam, with some suggestions,* Cambridge, 1819.

Jebb, E.   *Cambridge: a brief study in social questions,* Cambridge, 1906.

Jonas, S.   'On the Farming of Cambridgeshire', in *Journal of the Royal Agricultural Society* (VII), 1847.

Keynes, M.E.   *A House by the River: Newnham Grange to Darwin College,* Cambridge, 1976.

Kinderley, N.   *The Ancient and Present State of the Navigation of the Towns of Lynn, Wisbech, Spalding and Boston,* London, 1751.

Knight, F.   *University Rebel: the life of William Frend 1757-1841,* London, 1971.

    Letter to the Electors of Cambridge touching Mr. Knight, Mr. Sutton and the Poor Laws, Cambridge, 1837.

Lysons, D. and S.   *Magna Britannia,* 6 vols., London, 1806-22.

Maberly, F.H.   *To the Poor and their Friends, speeches, by F.H. Maberly, exhibiting the oppressive nature of the new Poor Law Amendment Act,* London, 1836.

Minnis, S.E.   *A Turbulent Priest*, n.d. but 195-.

Mullinger, J.B.   *A history of the University of Cambridge*, London, 1888.

Murphy, M.J.   'Newspapers and Opinion in Cambridge 1780-1850', in *Transactions of the Cambridge Bibliographic Society*, V, 1969-71.

Mutton, N.   'The use of steam drainage in the making of the Eau Brink Cut', in *Industrial Archaeology*, 4, 19€7.

Mylne, R.   *Report on the proposed Improvement of the drainage and navigation of the River Ouse*, London, 1792.

                      Narrative of the Celebration of Peace, Cambridge, 1814.

                      New Cambridge Guide(s) Cambridge 1812; 1830; 1868.

Nutter, B.   *The Story of the Cambridge Baptists*, Cambridge, 1912.

Okes, T.V.   *Observations upon the Fever lately prevalent at Cambridge*, Cambridge, 1815.

Page, T.H.   *Opinions upon the proposed cut from Eau Brink to Lynn*, London, 1793.

   "   *A Letter to Sir M. Folkes upon the Eau Brink Cut*, London, 1794.

Peacock, A.J.   *Bread or Blood: a study of the agrarian riots in East Anglia in 1816*, London, 1965.

Pryme, G.   *A Letter to the Freemen and Inhabitants of the town of Cambridge on the state of the borough*, Cambridge, 1823.

   "   *Obituary notice*, in *Cambridge Daily News*, 1869.

   "   *Autobiographic Recollections*, Cambridge, 1870.

Reeve, F.A.   *Cambridge*, London, 1964.

Roberts, S.C.   *The Evolution of Cambridge Publishing*, Cambridge, 1956.

Scott, E.   *A Plain Statement relative to the late Cambridge election petition*, Cambridge, 1840.

Scriblerus, M. (pseud.)	*The Ratland Feast: an historico-ludicro-comico poem,* Cambridge, 1820.
Sedgwick, A.	*Cambridge Petition on the abolition of religious tests in the University,* Cambridge, 1834.
Stokes, E.	'Cambridge Parish Workhouses', in *Proceedings of the Cambridge Antiquarian Society* (XLII), 1949.
Summers, D.	*The Great Ouse,* Newton Abbot, 1973.
Tate, W.E.	'Cambridgeshire Field Systems', in *Proceedings of the Cambridge Antiquarian Society* (XL), 1944.
Teichman, O.	*The Cambridge undergraduate 100 years ago,* Cambridge, 1926.
Vancouver, C.	*General View of the Agriculture in the County of Cambridge,* London, 1794.
	Victoria County History of Cambridgeshire and the Isle of Ely, 5 vols., London, 1938-1973.
Watté, J.	*Report for the better drainage of the South and Middle Levels of the Fens,* Cambridge, 1791.
Wells, S.	*The History of the drainage of the Great Level of the Fens, called the Bedford Level,* 2 vols., London, 1828-30.
Whittred, W.	*A Letter to the Freemen of the Corporation of Cambridge,* Cambridge, 1818.
Wildfire, M. (pseud.)	*Squibiana: a collection of addresses, songs and other effusions, published during the late election,* Cambridge, 1831.
Williams, B.	'The Eclipse of the Yorkes', in *Transactions of the Royal Historical Society,* 3rd Series vol. II, 1908.
Winstanley, D.A.	*Unreformed Cambridge: a study of certain aspects of the University in the eighteenth-century,* Cambridge, 1935.
"	*Early Victorian Cambridge,* Cambridge, 1940.

THE OLEANDER PRESS

A DICTIONARY OF COMMON FALLACIES
Philip Ward
Popular errors of antiquity and later times (including our
own) are anatomized with care and occasionally even
nostalgic affection.
THE GERMAN LEFT SINCE 1945
W.D. Graf
The socialist opposition in the Bundesrepublik since the
end of World War II, with a postscript by Ossip Flechtheim
of the Freie Universität, Berlin.
MARVELL'S ALLEGORICAL POETRY
Bruce King
Fresh light on the sources of Andrew Marvell's inspiration,
with new interpretations based on the poet's use of Biblical
theme and allegory.
CONTEMPORARY GERMAN POETRY
Ewald Osers
The eminent translator offers a personal anthology of major
poetry from West Germany, from Cibulka, Fried, and
Piontek, to Schäfer, Leisegang, Delius and Theobaldy.
BIOGRAPHICAL MEMOIRS OF EXTRAORDINARY
PAINTERS
William Beckford
The author of *Vathek* parodies the art books of his time in
a forgotten classic first published in 1780, now reissued in
facsimile with a new preface.
DIARY OF A JOURNEY ACROSS ARABIA
G.F. Sadleir
Arabia was crossed from east to west by a foreigner for the
first time in 1819. This is Sadleir's own account of the
expedition, with a new introduction.
THE LIBYAN REVOLUTION
I.M. Arif and M.O. Ansell
Legal and historical documents from the early days of the
new order in Libya, following the overthrow of King Idris I
on 1 September 1969, all in English.

The Oleander Press   The Oleander Press
17 Stansgate Avenue   210 Fifth Avenue
Cambridge CB2 2QZ   New York, N.Y. 10010
England.   U.S.A.

INDEX

101, 105
Reform Movement, 35, 60, 65, 75
Rennie, George, 80
Rennie, John, 46, 80
Revolution Society, 26
Ricardo, David, 69
Riot Act, 66
Riots, 13, 14, 35, 48, 50, 58, 66, 70, 79, 103
Robinson, Henry Crabb, 26
Robinson, *Rev.* Robert, 26, 39–41
Rochdale, 93
Roebuck, J.A., 114
Roman Catholics, 37, 64, 73
Romsey Town, 49
Round Church, 9
Royston, 11, 48, 82, 95
Russell, *Lord* John, 74–76
Rutland, *Duke of*, 35, 65–66, 68, 70, 96, 99. See also Manners, C.S.
Rutland Club, 35, 68

Sadler's Factory Report, 93
Saffron, 12, 13
Saffron Walden, 48
St. Thomas Leys, 49
Sawston, 58
Scotland, 29
Sedgwick, A., 98
Sheffield, 6, 24, 29
Sheffield Constitutional Society, 24, 33
Sheffield Independent, 26
Sheffield Reform Society, 33
Sheffield Register, 26, 32
Shepreth, 82
Shire Hall, 12, 78
Simeon, Charles, 36
'Six Acts', 59, 63
Slave trade, 26, 37–38, 41, 66
Slavery, abolition of, 66
Smith, Henry, 90–91
Smith, Sidney, 103
Society for Constitutional Information, 33
Society for the Suppression of Mendicity, 50
Society of the Friends of the People, 33
South Level, 43, 46–47
South Wales, 29
Spring-Rice, Thomas, 66, 77, 100–101
Stamford, 15
Stamford Mercury, 111
Stamp Duty, 19, 20, 24. See also Appendix C.

Stanhope, *Lord*, 18
Star and Garter', 'The, 100
Stephen, Leslie, 8
St[o]urbridge Fair, 10–11
Suffolk Chronicle, 19
Sugden, *Sir* Edward, 67
Sunday School Movement, 79
Sutton, Manners C., 100

Tamworth Manifesto, 104
Taylor, J.E. (editor of *Manchester Guardian*), 26
Telford, Thomas, 46
Ten Hours Bill, 94
Test & Corporation Acts, 15, 36
Thackeray, *Dr.*, 50, 82
Thames, River, 10, 47
Thornton, Henry, 38
Times, The, 6, 19, 72, 77, 94, 96, 98
Tiverton, 29, 111
Tolls Case, 67
Tories, and *Cambridge Chronicle*, 24–25, 59–60, 90, 113, 115; and *Cambridge Journal and Weekly Flying Post*, 16; and *Cambridge Weekly Journal*, 71; and Cambridge University, 14, 70, 72; and Catholic Question, 69–70, 72; and the Church, 98–99; and Corn Laws, 102–103; and education, 98, 99; and electoral bribery, 100–101; and Peel, 104; and Poor Law, 94, 96; and reform, 69–70; and Reform Bill, 93. See also Conservatives.
Townley, Richard Greaves, 76–77, 103
Trade, River-borne, 11–12, 46, 83
Trade Unions, 112
Trench, *Colonel*, 65, 70, 72
Triumvirate, 34
Trumpington Road, 49
Trumpington Street, 9, 11
Turnpike Trusts, 10

Unitarians, 15, 26, 30, 36–40. See also Dissenters.
Universal suffrage, 63
University, *see* Cambridge University

Vaccination, 50
Vagrants, 11, 50
Vancouver, Charles, 12, 48
Vermuyden, Cornelius, 43
Victoria, *Queen*, 13

CAMBRIDGE TOWN, GOWN, AND COUNTY